IOLÄUS

PREFACE TO FIRST EDITION

THE degree to which Friendship, in the early history of the world, has been recognised as an institution, and the dignity ascribed to it, are things hardly realized to-day. Yet a very slight examination of the subject shows the important part it has played. In making the following collection I have been much struck by the remarkable manner in which the customs of various races and times illustrate each other, and the way in which they point to a solid and enduring body of human sentiment on the subject. By arranging the extracts in a kind of rough chronological and evolutionary order from those dealing with primitive races onwards, the continuity of these customs comes out all the more clearly, as well as their slow modification in course of time. But it must be confessed that the present collection is only incomplete, and a small contribution, at best, towards a large subject.

In the matter of quotation and translation, my best thanks are due to various authors and holders of literary copyrights for their assistance and authority; and especially to the Master and Fellows of Balliol College for permission to quote from the late Professor Jowett's translation of Plato's dia-

logues ; to Messrs. George Bell & Sons for leave
to make use of the Bohn series; to Messrs. A. & C.
Black for leave of quotation from the late J. Addington Symonds' *Studies of the Greek Poets ;* and
to Messrs. Longmans, Green & Co., for sanction
of extracts from the Rev. W. H. Hutchings' translation of the *Confessions of St. Augustine.* In cases
where no reference is given the translations are by
the Editor.

E. C.

March, 1902.

CONTENTS

"*And as to the loves of Hercules it is difficult to record them because of their number   But some who think that Ioläus was one of them, do to this day worship and honour him ; and make their loved ones swear fidelity at his tomb.*"

(*Plutarch*)

I.

Friendship-Customs
in the Pagan & Early World

Friendship-Customs
in the Pagan & Early World

FRIENDSHIP-CUSTOMS, of a very marked and definite character, have apparently prevailed among a great many primitive peoples; but the information that we have about them is seldom thoroughly satisfactory. Travellers have been content to note external ceremonies, like the exchange of names between comrades, or the mutual tasting of each other's blood, but—either from want of perception or want of opportunity—have not been able to tell us anything about the inner meaning of these formalities, or the sentiments which may have inspired them. Still, we have material enough to indicate that comrade-attachment has been recognised as an important institution, and held in high

3

esteem, among quite savage tribes ; and some of the following quotations will show this. When we come to the higher culture of the Greek age the material fortunately is abundant—not only for the customs, but (in Greek philosophy and poetry) for the inner sentiments which inspired these customs. Consequently it will be found that the major part of this and the following two chapters deals with matter from Greek sources. The later chapters carry on the subject in loosely historical sequence through the Christian centuries down to modern times.

HE Balonda are an African tribe inhabiting Londa land, among the Southern tributaries of the Congo River. They were visited by Livingstone, and the following account of their customs is derived from him :—

"THE Balonda have a most remarkable custom of cementing friendship. When two men agree to be special friends they go through a singular ceremony. The men sit opposite each other holding hands, and by the side of each is a vessel

4

of beer. Slight cuts are then made on the clasped *Primitive* hands, on the pit of the stomach, on the right *Ceremony* cheek, and on the forehead. The point of a grass-blade is pressed against each of these cuts, so as to take up a little of the blood, and each man washes the grass-blade in his own beer vessel. The vessels are then exchanged and the contents drunk, so that each imbibes the blood of the other. The two are thenceforth considered as blood-relations, and are bound to assist each other in every possible manner. While the beer is being drunk, the friends of each of the men beat on the ground with clubs, and bawl out certain sentences as ratification of the treaty. It is thought correct for all the friends of each party to the contract to drink a little of the beer. The ceremony is called 'Kasendi.' After it has been completed, gifts are exchanged, and both parties always give their most precious possessions." *Natural History of Man. Rev. J. G. Wood. Vol: Africa*, p. 419.

Among the Manganjas and other tribes of the Zambesi region, Livingstone found the custom of changing names prevalent.

"SININYANE (a headman) had exchanged names with a Zulu at Shupanga, and on being called the next morning made no answer; to a

second and third summons he paid no attention;
but at length one of his men replied, 'He is not
Sininyane now, he is Moshoshoma;' and to this
name he answered promptly. The custom of ex-
changing names with men of other tribes is not
uncommon ; and the exchangers regard themselves as close comrades, owing special duties to
each other ever after. Should one by chance visit
his comrade's town, he expects to receive food,
lodging, and other friendly offices from him."
*Narrative of an Expedition to the Zambesi. By
David and Charles Livingstone. Murray, 1865,
p. 148.*

IN the story of David and Jonathan,
which follows, we have an example,
from much the same stage of primitive
tribal life, of a compact between two
friends—one the son of the chief, the other a shepherd youth—only in this case, in the song of
David ("I am distressed for thee, my brother Jonathan, thy love to me was wonderful") we are for-
tunate in having the inner feeling preserved for us.
It should be noted that Jonathan gives to David
his "most precious possessions."

6

" AND when Saul saw David go forth against *David an*
the Philistine (Goliath), he said unto Abner, *Jonathan*
the captain of the host, 'Abner, whose son is this
youth?' And Abner said, 'As thy soul liveth, O
King, I cannot tell.' And the King said, 'Inquire
thou whose son the stripling is.' And as David
returned from the slaughter of the Philistine,
Abner took him and brought him before Saul,
with the head of the Philistine in his hand. And
Saul said to him, 'Whose son art thou, young
man?' And David answered, 'The son of thy
servant Jesse the Bethlehemite.'

"And it came to pass, when he had made an
end of speaking unto Saul, that the soul of Jonathan
was knit with the soul of David, and Jonathan
loved him as his own soul. And Saul took him
that day, and would let him go no more home to
his father's house. Then Jonathan and David
made a covenant, because he loved him as his own
soul. And Jonathan stripped himself of the robe
that was upon him, and gave it to David, and his
garments, even to his sword, and to his bow, and
to his girdle." 1 *Sam.* ch. xvii. 55.

With regard to the exchange of names, a slightly *Flower*
different custom prevails among the Bengali coolies. *Friends*
Two youths, or two girls, will exchange two

7

flowers (of the same kind) with each other, in token of perpetual alliance. After that, one speaks of the other as "my flower," but never alludes to the other by *name* again—only by some round-about phrase.

HERMAN MELVILLE, who voyaged among the Pacific Islands in 1841-1845, gives some interesting and reliable accounts of Polynesian customs of that period. He says :—

Polynesia
Tahiti
"THE really curious way in which all the Polynesians are in the habit of making bosom friends at the shortest possible notice is deserving of remark. Although, among a people like the Tahitians, vitiated as they are by sophisticating influences, this custom has in most cases degenerated into a mere mercenary relation, it nevertheless had its origin in a fine, and in some instances heroic, sentiment formerly entertained by their fathers.

"In the annals of the island (Tahiti) are examples of extravagant friendships, unsurpassed by the story of Damon and Pythias, in truth, much more wonderful ; for notwithstanding the devotion—even of life in some cases—to which they

8

led, they were frequently entertained at first sight for some stranger from another island." *Omoo, Herman Melville*, ch. 39, p. 154.

"THOUGH little inclined to jealousy in (ordinary) love-matters, the Tahitian will hear of no rivals in his friendship." *Ibid*, ch. 40.

Melville spent some months on one of the Marquesas Islands, in a valley occupied by a tribe called Typees; one day there turned up a stranger belonging to a hostile tribe who occupied another part of the island:—

"THE stranger could not have been more than *Marquesas* twenty-five years of age, and was a little *Islands* above the ordinary height; had he been a single hair's breadth taller, the matchless symmetry of his form would have been destroyed. His unclad limbs were beautifully formed; whilst the elegant outline of his figure, together with his beardless cheeks, might have entitled him to the distinction of standing for the statue of the Polynesian Apollo; and indeed the oval of his countenance and the regularity of every feature reminded me of an antique bust. But the marble repose of art was supplied by a warmth and liveliness of expression only to be seen in the South Sea Islander

9

under the most favourable developments of nature. . . . When I expressed my surprise (at his venturing among the Typees) he looked at me for a moment as if enjoying my perplexity, and then with his strange vivacity exclaimed—'Ah! me taboo—me go Nukuheva—me go Tior—me go Typee—me go everywhere—nobody harm me, me taboo.'

"This explanation would have been altogether unintelligible to me, had it not recalled to my mind something I had previously heard concerning a singular custom among these islanders. Though the country is possessed by various tribes, whose mutual hostilities almost wholly preclude any intercourse between them; yet there are instances where a person having ratified friendly relations with some individual belonging to the valley, whose inmates are at war with his own, may under particular restrictions venture with impunity into the country of his friend, where under other circumstances he would have been treated as an enemy. In this light are personal friendships regarded among them, and the individual so protected is said to be 'taboo,' and his person to a certain extent is held as sacred. Thus the stranger informed me he had access to all the valleys in the island." *Typee, Herman Melville*, ch. xviii.

Pagan & Early World

IN almost all primitive nations, warfare has given rise to institutions of military comradeship—including, for instance, institutions of instruction for young warriors, of personal devotion to their leaders, or of personal attachment to each other. In Greece these customs were specially defined, as later quotations will show.

Tacitus, speaking of the arrangement among the Germans by which each military chief was surrounded by younger companions in arms, says:—

"THERE is great emulation among the companions, which shall possess the highest place in the favour of their chief; and among the chiefs, which shall excel in the number and valour of his companions. It is their dignity, their strength, to be always surrounded with a large body of select youth, an ornament in peace, a bulwark in war . . . In the field of battle, it is disgraceful for the chief to be surpassed in valour; it is disgraceful for the companions not to equal their chief; but it is reproach and infamy during a whole succeeding life to retreat from the field surviving him. To aid, to protect him; to place their own

Tacitus on Military Comradeship

gallant actions to the account of his glory is their first and most sacred engagement." *Tacitus, Germania,* 13, 14, *Bohn Series.*

AMONG the Arab tribes very much the same thing may be found, every Sheikh having his bodyguard of young men, whom he instructs and educates, while they render to him their military and personal devotion. In the late expedition of the British to Khartoum (Nov., 1899), when Colonel Wingate and his troops mowed down the Khalifa and his followers with their Maxims, the death of the Khalifa was thus described by a correspondent of the daily papers :—

The "IN the centre of what was evidently the main
Khalifa at attack on our right we came across a very large
Khartoum number of bodies all huddled together in a very small place ; their horses lay dead behind them, the Khalifa lay dead on his furma, or sheepskin, the typical end of the Arab Sheikh who disdains surrender ; on his right was the Khalifa Aly Wad Hila, and on his left Ahmed Fedil, his great fighting leader, whilst all around him lay his faithful emirs, all content to meet their death when he had chosen

to meet his. His black Mulamirin, or bodyguard, all lay dead in a straight line about 40 yards in front of their master's body, with their faces to the foe and faithful to the last. It was truly a touching sight, and one could not help but feel that. . . their end was truly grand. . . . . Amongst the dead were found two men tied together by the arms, who had charged towards the guns and had got nearer than any others. On enquiring of the prisoners Colonel Wingate was told these two were great friends, and on seeing the Egyptian guns come up had tied themselves by the arms with a cord, swearing to reach the guns or die together."

Compare also the following quotation from Ammianus Marcellinus (xvi. 13), who says that when Chonodomarus, "King of the Alamanni," was taken prisoner by the Romans,

"HIS companions, two hundred in number, and *Primitive* three friends peculiarly attached to him, *Germans* thinking it infamous to survive their prince, or not to die for him, surrendered themselves to be put in bonds."

The following passage from Livingstone shows the existence among the African tribes of his time of a system, which Wood rightly says "has a singular resemblance to the instruction of pages in the days of chivalry":—

South
African
Tribes

"MONINA (one of the confederate chiefs of the Banyai) had a great number of young men about him, from twelve to fifteen years of age. These were all sons of free men, and bands of young lads like them in the different districts leave their parents about the age of puberty and live with such men as Monina for the sake of instruction. When I asked the nature of the instruction I was told 'Bonyái,' which I suppose may be understood as indicating manhood, for it sounds as if we should say, 'to teach an American Americanism,' or, 'an Englishman to be English.' While here they are kept in subjection to rather stringent regulations. . . . . They remain unmarried until a fresh set of youths is ready to occupy their place under the same instruction." *Missionary Travels and Researches in South Africa. By David Livingstone,* 1857, p. 618.

M. Foley (Bulln. Soc. d'Anthr. de Paris, 1879) speaks of fraternity in arms among the natives of New Caledonia as forming a close tie—closer even than consanguinity.

Pagan & Early World

WITH regard to Greece, J. Addington
Symonds has some interesting remarks, which are well worthy of
consideration; he says:—

"NEARLY all the historians of Greece have *Greek*
failed to insist upon the fact that fraternity in *Friendship*
arms played for the Greek race the same part as the *and*
idealisation of women for the knighthood of feudal *Mediæval*
Europe. Greek mythology and history are full of *Chivalry*
tales of friendship, which can only be paralleled by
the story of David and Jonathan in the Bible. The
legends of Herakles and Hylas, of Theseus and
Peirithous, of Apollo and Hyacinth, of Orestes and
Pylades, occur immediately to the mind. Among
the noblest patriots, tyrannicides, lawgivers, and
self-devoted heroes in the early times of Greece,
we always find the names of friends and comrades
received with peculiar honour. Harmodius and
Aristogeiton, who slew the despot Hipparchus at
Athens; Diocles and Philolaus, who gave laws to
Thebes; Chariton and Melanippus, who resisted
the sway of Phalaris in Sicily; Cratinus and Aristo-
demus, who devoted their lives to propitiate offended deities when a plague had fallen on Athens;
these comrades, staunch to each other in their love,

and elevated by friendship to the pitch of noblest enthusiasm, were among the favourite saints of Greek legend and history. In a word, the chivalry of Hellas found its motive force in friendship rather than in the love of women; and the motive force of all chivalry is a generous, soul-exalting, unselfish passion. The fruit which friendship bore among the Greeks was courage in the face of danger, indifference to life when honour was at stake, patriotic ardour, the love of liberty, and lion-hearted rivalry in battle. 'Tyrants,' said Plato, 'stand in awe of friends.'" *Studies of the Greek Poets. By J. A. Symonds*, vol. 1, p. 97.

HE customs connected with this fraternity in arms, in Sparta and in Crete, are described with care and at considerable length in the following extract from Müller's *History and Antiquities of the Doric Race*, book iv., ch. 4, par. 6:—

"AT Sparta the party loving was called εἰσπνήλας, and his affection was termed a *breathing in*, or *inspiring* (εἰσπνεῖν); which expresses the pure and mental connection between the two persons, and corresponds with the name of the other, viz.: ἀίτας, i.e., *listener* or *hearer*. Now it appears to have been the practice for every youth of good character to have his lover; and on the other hand every well-educated man was bound by custom to be the lover of some youth. Instances of this connection are furnished by several of the royal family of Sparta; thus, Agesilaus, while he still belonged to the herd (ἀγέλη) of youths, was the hearer (ἀίτας) of Lysander, and himself had in his turn also a hearer; his son Archidamus was the lover of the son of Sphodrias, the noble Cleonymus; Cleomenes III. was when a young man the hearer of Xenares, and later in life the lover of the brave Panteus. The connection usually originated from the proposal of the lover; yet it was necessary that the listener should accept him with real affection, as a regard to the riches of the proposer was considered very disgraceful; sometimes, however, it happened that the proposal originated from the other party. The connection appears to have been very intimate and faithful; and was recognised by the State. If his relations were absent, the youth might be represented in the public assembly by his lover; in battle too they stood near one another, where their fidelity and affection were often shown till death; while at home the youth was constantly under the eyes of his lover, who was to him as it were a model and pattern of life; which explains why, for many

Fraternity in Arms in Spain

17

faults, particularly want of ambition, the lover could be punished instead of the listener."

Crete "THIS ancient national custom prevailed with still greater force in Crete; which island was hence by many persons considered as the original seat of the connection in question. Here too it was disgraceful for a well-educated youth to be without a lover; and hence the party loved was termed κλεινὸς, the *praised*; the lover being simply called φιλήτωρ. It appears that the youth was always carried away by force, the intention of the ravisher being previously communicated to the relations, who however took no measures of precaution, and only made a feigned resistance; except when the ravisher appeared, either in family or talent, unworthy of the youth. The lover then led him away to his apartment (ἀνδρεῖον), and afterwards, with any chance companions, either to the mountains or to his estate. Here they remained two months (the period prescribed by custom), which were passed chiefly in hunting together. After this time had expired, the lover dismissed the youth, and at his departure gave him, according to custom, an ox, a military dress, and brazen cup, with other things; and frequently these gifts were increased by the friends of the ravisher. The youth then sacrificed the ox to Jupiter, with which he gave a feast

18

to his companions : and now he stated how he had been pleased with his lover; and he had complete liberty by law to punish any insult or disgraceful treatment. It depended now on the choice of the youth whether the connection should be broken off or not. If it was kept up, the companion in arms (παραστάτης), as the youth was then called, wore the military dress which had been given him, and fought in battle next his lover, inspired with double valour by the gods of war and love, according to the notions of the Cretans; and even in man's age he was distinguished by the first place and rank in the course, and certain insignia worn about the body.

"Institutions, so systematic and regular as these, did not exist in any Doric State except Crete and Sparta; but the feelings on which they were founded seem to have been common to all the Dorians. The loves of Philolaus, a Corinthian of the family of the Bacchiadae, and the lawgiver of Thebes, and of Diocles the Olympic conqueror, lasted until death; and even their graves were turned towards one another in token of their affection; and another person of the same name was honoured in Megara, as a noble instance of self-devotion for the object of his love." *Ibid.*

For an account of Philolaus and Diocles, Aris-

19

totle (Pol. ii. 9) may be referred to. The second Diocles was an Athenian who died in battle for the youth he loved.

Diocles "HIS tomb was honoured with the ἐναγίσματα of heroes, and a yearly contest for skill in kissing formed part of his memorial celebration." *J. A. Symonds'* "*A Problem in Greek Ethics*," *privately printed,* 1883 ; *see also Theocritus,* Idyll xii. infra.

HAHN, in his *Albanesische Studien,* says that the Dorian customs of comradeship still flourish in Albania "just as described by the ancients," and are closely entwined with the whole life of the people —though he says nothing of any military signification. It appears to be a quite recognised institution for a young man to take to himself a youth or boy as his special comrade. He instructs, and when necessary reproves, the younger ; protects him, and makes him presents of various kinds. The relation generally, though not always ends with the marriage of the elder. The following is reported by Hahn as in the actual words of his informant (an Albanian) :—

Pagan & Early World

"LOVE of this kind is occasioned by the sight *Albanian* of a beautiful youth; who thus kindles in *Customs* the lover a feeling of wonder and causes his heart to open to the sweet sense which springs from the contemplation of beauty. By degrees love steals in and takes possession of the lover, and to such a degree that all his thoughts and feelings are absorbed in it. When near the beloved he loses himself in the sight of him; when absent he thinks of him only." These loves, he continued, "are with a few exceptions as pure as sunshine, and the highest and noblest affections that the human heart can entertain." *Hahn*, vol. 1, p. 166.

Hahn also mentions that troops of youths, like the Cretan and Spartan *agelae*, are formed in Albania, of twenty-five or thirty members each. The comradeship usually begins during adolescence, each member paying a fixed sum into a common fund, and the interest being spent on two or three annual feasts, generally held out of doors.

THE Sacred Band of Thebes, or Theban Band, was a battalion composed entirely of friends and lovers; and forms a remarkable example of mili-

21

tary comradeship. The references to it in later Greek literature are very numerous, and there seems no reason to doubt the general truth of the traditions concerning its formation and its complete annihilation by Philip of Macedon at the battle of Chaeronea (B. C. 338). Thebes was the last stronghold of Hellenic independence, and with the Theban Band Greek freedom perished. But the mere existence of this phalanx, and the fact of its renown, show to what an extent comradeship was recognised and prized as an *institution* among these peoples. The following account is taken from Plutarch's *Life of Pelopidas*, Clough's translation :—

The Theban Band "GORGIDAS, according to some, first formed the Sacred Band of 300 chosen men, to whom as being a guard for the citadel the State allowed provision, and all things necessary for exercise; and hence they were called the city band, as citadels of old were usually called cities. Others say that it was composed of young men attached to each other by personal affection, and a pleasant saying of Pammenes is current, that Homer's Nestor was not well skilled in ordering an army, when he advised the Greeks to rank tribe and tribe, and family and family, together, that so 'tribe might tribe, and kinsmen kinsmen aid,' but that he should have joined lovers and their beloved. For men of the same tribe or family little value one another when dangers press; but a band cemented together by friendship grounded upon love is never to be broken, and invincible; since the lovers, ashamed to be base in sight of their beloved, and the beloved before their lovers, willingly rush into danger for the relief of one another. Nor can that be wondered at since they have more regard for their absent lovers than for others present; as in the instance of the man who, when his enemy was going to kill him, earnestly requested him to run him through the breast, that his lover might not blush to see him wounded in the back. It is a tradition likewise that Ioläus, who assisted Hercules in his labours and fought at his side, was beloved of him; and Aristotle observes that even in his time lovers plighted their faith at Ioläus' tomb. It is likely, therefore, that this band was called sacred on this account; as Plato calls a lover a divine friend. It is stated that it was never beaten till the battle at Chaeronea; and when Philip after the fight took a view of the slain, and came to the place where the three hundred that fought his phalanx lay dead together, he wondered, and understanding

The   that it was the band of lovers, he shed tears and
Theban said, 'Perish any man who suspects that these men
Band   either did or suffered anything that was base.'

"It was not the disaster of Laius, as the poets imagine, that first gave rise to this form of attachment
among the Thebans, but their law-givers, design-
ing to soften whilst they were young their natural
fickleness, brought for example the pipe into great
esteem, both in serious and sportive occasions, and
gave great encouragement to these friendships in
the Palaestra, to temper the manner and character
of the youth. With a view to this, they did well
again to make Harmony, the daughter of Mars
and Venus, their tutelar deity; since where force
and courage is joined with gracefulness and winning behaviour, a harmony ensues that combines
all the elements of society in perfect consonance
and order.

"Gorgidas distributed this sacred Band all
through the front ranks of the infantry, and thus
made their gallantry less conspicuous; not being
united in one body, but mingled with many others
of inferior resolution, they had no fair opportunity
of showing what they could do. But Pelopidas,
having sufficiently tried their bravery at Tegyrae,
where they had fought alone, and around his own
person, never afterwards divided them, but keep-

ing them entire, and as one man, gave them the first duty in the greatest battles. For as horses run brisker in a chariot than single, not that their joint force divides the air with greater ease, but because being matched one against another circulation kindles and enflames their courage; thus, he thought, brave men, provoking one another to noble actions, would prove most serviceable and most resolute where all were united together."

STORIES of romantic friendship form a staple subject of Greek literature, and were everywhere accepted and prized. The following quotations from Athenæus and Plutarch contain allusions to the Theban Band, and other examples :—

"AND the Lacedæmonians offer sacrifices to *Athenæus* Love before they go to battle, thinking that safety and victory depend on the friendship of those who stand side by side in the battle array. ... And the regiment among the Thebans, which is called the *Sacred Band*, is wholly composed of mutual lovers, indicating the majesty of the God, as these men prefer a glorious death to a shameful and discreditable life." *Athenæus*, bk. xiii., ch. 12.

Ioläus, above-mentioned, is said to have been the

charioteer of Hercules, and his faithful companion. As the comrade of Hercules he was worshipped beside him in Thebes, where the gymnasium was named after him. Plutarch alludes to this friendship again in his treatise on Love (*Eroticus*, par. 17) :—

Ioläus " AND as to the loves of Hercules, it is difficult to record them because of their number ; but those who think that Ioläus was one of them do to this day worship and honour him, and make their loved ones swear fidelity at his tomb."

And in the same treatise :—

Plutarch on Love "CONSIDER also how Love (Eros) excels in warlike feats, and is by no means idle, as Euripides called him, nor a carpet knight, nor 'sleeping on soft maidens' cheeks.' For a man inspired by Love needs not Ares to help him when he goes out as a warrior against the enemy, but at the bidding of his own god is 'ready' for his friend 'to go through fire and water and whirlwinds.' And in Sophocles' play, when the sons of Niobe are being shot at and dying, one of them calls out for no helper or assister but his lover.

"And you know of course how it was that Cleomachus, the Pharsalian, fell in battle. . . . When the war between the Eretrians and Chalcidians was at its height, Cleomachus had come to aid the latter with a Thessalian force; and the Chalcidian infantry seemed strong enough, but they had great difficulty in repelling the enemy's cavalry. So they begged that high-souled hero, Cleomachus, to charge the Eretrian cavalry first. And he asked the youth he loved, who was by, if he would be a spectator of the fight, and he saying he would, and affectionately kissing him and putting his helmet on his head, Cleomachus, with a proud joy, put himself at the head of the bravest of the Thessalians, and charged the enemy's cavalry with such impetuosity that he threw them into disorder and routed them; and the Eretrian infantry also fleeing in consequence, the Chalcidians won a splendid victory. However, Cleomachus got killed, and they show his tomb in the market place at Chalcis, over which a huge pillar stands to this day." *Eroticus*, par. 17, *trans. Bohn's Classics.*

And further on in the same :—

" AND among you Thebans, Pemptides, is it not usual for the lover to give his boylove a complete suit of armour when he is enrolled among the men ? And did not the erotic Pammenes change the disposition of the heavy-armed infantry, censuring Homer as knowing nothing about love, because he drew up the Achæans in order of battle in tribes and clans, and did not put lover and love together, that so 'spear should be next to spear and helmet to helmet' (*Iliad*, xiii. 131), seeing that love is the only invincible general. For men in battle will leave in the lurch clansmen and friends, aye, and parents and sons, but what warrior ever broke through or charged through lover and love, seeing that when there is no necessity lovers frequently display their bravery and contempt of life."

Athenæus on the same

THE following is from the *Deipnosophists* of Athenæus (bk. xiii. ch. 78):—

"BUT Hieronymus the Peripatetic says that the loves of youths used to be much encouraged, for this reason, that the vigour of the young and their close agreement in comradeship have led to the overthrow of many a tyranny. For in the presence of his favorite a lover would rather endure anything than earn the name of coward ; a thing which was proved in practice by the Sacred Band, established at Thebes under Epaminondas ; as well as by the death of the Pisistratidæ, which was brought about by Harmodius and Aristogeiton.

"And at Agrigentum in Sicily the same was shown by the mutual love of Chariton and Melanippus—of whom Melanippus was the younger beloved, as Heraclides of Pontus tells in his Treatise on Love. For these two having been accused of plotting against Phalaris, and being put to torture in order to force them to betray their accomplices, not only did not tell, but even compelled Phalaris to such pity of their tortures that he released them with many words of praise. Whereupon Apollo, pleased at his conduct, granted to Phalaris a respite from death ; and declared the same to the men who inquired of the Pythian priestess how they might best attack him. He also gave an oracular saying concerning Chariton . . . .

'Blessed indeed was Chariton and Melanippus,
    Pioneers of Godhead, and of mortals the one
    most* beloved.'"

Epaminondas, the great Theban general and statesman, so we are told by the same author, had for his young comrades Asopichus and Cephisodorus, "the latter of whom fell with him at Mantineia, and is buried near him."

*This curious oracle seems purposely to confuse the singular and plural.

29

THESE are mainly instances of what might be called "military comradeship," but as may be supposed, friendship in the early world did not rest on this alone. With the growth of culture other interests came in; and among the Greeks especially association in the pursuit of art or politics or philosophy became a common ground. Parmenides, the philosopher, whose life was held peculiarly holy, loved his pupil Zeno (see Plato *Parm*, 127A):

*Parmen-
ides and
Zeno*

"**P**ARMENIDES and Zeno came to Athens, he said, at the great Panathenæan festival; the former was, at the time of his visit, about 65 years old, very white with age, but well-favoured. Zeno was nearly 40 years of age, of a noble figure and fair aspect; and in the days of his youth he was reported to have been beloved of Parmenides."

Pheidias, the sculptor, loved Pantarkes, a youth of Elis, and carved his portrait at the foot of the Olympian Zeus (Pausanias v. 11), and politicians and orators like Demosthenes and Æschines were proud to avow their attachments. It was in a house

of ill-fame, according to Diogenes Laertius (ii. 105)
that Socrates first met Phædo :—

"THIS unfortunate youth was a native of Elis. *Phædo*
Taken prisoner in war, he was sold in the
public market to a slave dealer, who then acquired
the right by Attic law to engross his earnings for
his own pocket. A friend of Socrates, perhaps
Cebes, bought him from his master, and he became
one of the chief members of the Socratic circle. His
name is given to the Platonic dialogue on immortality, and he lived to found what is called the
Eleo-Socratic School. No reader of Plato forgets
how the sage on the eve of his death stroked the
beautiful long hair of Phædo, and prophesied that
he would soon have to cut it short in mourning for
his teacher." *J. A. Symonds, A Problem in Greek
Ethics* p. 58.

The relation of friendship to the pursuit of philosophy is a favorite subject with Plato, and is illustrated by some later quotations (see *infra* ch. 2).

CONCLUDE the present section by
the insertion of three stories taken
from classical sources. Though of
a legendary character, it is probable
that they enshrine some memory or tradition of

actual facts. The story of Harmodius and Aristogeiton at any rate is treated by Herodotus and
Thucydides as a matter of serious history. The
names of these two friends were ever on the lips of
the Athenians as the founders of the city's freedom,
and to be born of their blood was esteemed among
the highest of honours. But whether historical or
not, these stories have much the same value for us,
in so far as they indicate the ideals on which the
Greek mind dwelt, and which it considered possible
of realisation.

*The Story
of Harmo-
dius and
Aristo-
geiton*

"NOW the attempt of Aristogeiton and Harmodius arose out of a love affair, which I will
narrate at length; and the narrative will show that
the Athenians themselves give quite an inaccurate
account of their own tyrants, and of the incident
in question, and know no more than other Hel-
lenes. Pisistratus died at an advanced age in possession of the tyranny, and then, not as is the
common opinion Hipparchus, but Hippias (who
was the eldest of his sons) succeeded to his power.

"Harmodius was in the flower of his youth, and
Aristogeiton, a citizen of the middle class, became
his lover. Hipparchus made an attempt to gain

the affections of Harmodius, but he would not listen to him, and told Aristogeiton. The latter was naturally tormented at the idea, and fearing that Hipparchus, who was powerful, would resort to violence, at once formed such a plot as a man in his station might for the overthrow of the tyranny. Meanwhile Hipparchus made another attempt; he had no better success, and thereupon he determined, not indeed to take any violent step, but to insult Harmodius in some underhand manner, so that his motive could not be suspected.[a] . . .

"When Hipparchus found his advances repelled by Harmodius he carried out his intention of insulting him. There was a young sister of his whom Hipparchus and his friends first invited to come and carry a sacred basket in a procession, and then rejected her, declaring that she had never been invited by them at all because she was unworthy. At this Harmodius was very angry, and Aristogeiton for his sake more angry still. They and the other conspirators had already laid their preparations, but were waiting for the festival of the great Panathenæa, when the citizens who took part in the procession assembled in arms; for to wear arms on any other day would have aroused suspicion. Harmodius and Aristogeiton were to begin the attack, and the rest were immediately to

[a] Digression in praise of the political administration of the Pisistratidæ

join in, and engage with the guards. The plot had been communicated to a few only, the better to avoid detection; but they hoped that, however few struck the blow, the crowd who would be armed, although not in the secret, would at once rise and assist in the recovery of their own liberties.

"The day of the festival arrived, and Hippias went out of the city to the place called the Ceramicus, where he was occupied with his guards in marshalling the procession. Harmodius and Aristogeiton, who were ready with their daggers, stepped forward to do the deed. But seeing one of the conspirators in familiar conversation with Hippias, who was readily accessible to all, they took alarm and imagined that they had been betrayed, and were on the point of being seized. Whereupon they determined to take their revenge first on the man who had outraged them and was the cause of their desperate attempt. So they rushed, just as they were, within the gates. They found Hipparchus near the Leocorium, as it was called, and then and there falling upon him with all the blind fury, one of an injured lover, the other of a man smarting under an insult, they smote and slew him. The crowd ran together, and so Aristogeiton for the present escaped the guards; but he was afterwards taken, and not very gently handled

34

(*i.e., tortured*). Harmodius perished on the spot."
Thuc: vi. 54-56, *trans. by B. Jowett.*

"PHOCIS preserves from early times the memory of the union between Orestes and Pylades, who taking a god as witness of the passion between them, sailed through life together as though in one boat. Both together put to death Klytemnestra, as though both were sons of Agamemnon; and Ægisthus was slain by both. Pylades suffered more than his friend by the punishment which pursued Orestes. He stood by him when condemned, nor did they limit their tender friendship by the bounds of Greece, but sailed to the furthest boundaries of the Scythians—the one sick, the other ministering to him. When they had come into the Tauric land straightway they were met by the matricidal fury; and while the barbarians were standing round in a circle Orestes fell down and lay on the ground, seized by his usual mania, while Pylades 'wiped away the foam, tended his body, and covered him with his well-woven cloak'—acting not only like a lover but like a father.

"When it was determined that one should remain to be put to death, and the other should go to Mycenæ to convey a letter, each wishes to remain for the sake of the other, thinking that if he saves the life of his friend he saves his own life. Orestes re-

The Story of Orestes and Pylades

35

fused to take the letter, saying that Pylades was more worthy to carry it, acting more like the lover than the beloved. 'For,' he said, 'the slaying of this man would be a great grief to me, as I am the cause of these misfortunes.' And he added, 'Give the tablet to him, for (turning to Pylades) I will send thee to Argos, in order that it may be well with thee; as for me, let anyone kill me who desires it.'

"Such love is always like that; for when from boyhood a serious love has grown up and it becomes adult at the age of reason, the long-loved object returns reciprocal affection, and it is hard to determine which is the lover of which, for—as from a mirror—the affection of the lover is reflected from the beloved." *Trans. from Lucian's Amores, by W. J. Baylis.*

"DAMON and Phintias, initiates in the Pythagorean mysteries, contracted so faithful a friendship towards each other, that when Dionysius of Syracuse intended to execute one of them, and he had obtained permission from the tyrant to return home and arrange his affairs before his death, the other did not hesitate to give himself up as a pledge of his friend's return.[a] He whose neck had been in danger was now free; and he who might have lived in safety was now in danger of death. So everybody, and especially Dionysius, were won-

[a] "For the two men lived together, and had their possessions in common." *Iamblichus, de Vita Pythagoræ* bk. i. ch. 33.

dering what would be the upshot of this novel and dubious affair. At last, when the day fixed was close at hand, and he had not returned, everyone condemned the one who stood security, for his stupidity and rashness. But he insisted that he had nothing to fear in the matter of his friend's constancy. And indeed at the same moment and the hour fixed by Dionysius, he who had received leave, returned. The tyrant, admiring the courage of both, remitted the sentence which had so tried their loyalty, and asked them besides to receive him in the bonds of their friendship, saying that he would make his third place in their affection agreeable by his utmost goodwill and effort. Such indeed are the powers of friendship: to breed contempt of death, to overcome the sweet desire of life, to humanise cruelty, to turn hate into love, to compensate punishment by largess; to which powers almost as much veneration is due as to the cult of the immortal gods. For if with these rests the public safety, on those does private happiness depend; and as the temples are the sacred domiciles of these, so of those are the loyal hearts of men as it were the shrines consecrated by some holy spirit." *Valerius Maximus*, bk. iv. ch. 7. *De Amicitiæ Vinculo.*

The Story of Damon and Pythias (or Phintias)

37

II.

The Place of Friendship in Greek Life & Thought

Strength, because by the recognition everywhere of romantic comradeship, public and private life was filled by a kind of divine fire ; weakness, because by the non-recognition of woman's equal part in such comradeship, her saving, healing, and redeeming influence was lost, and the Greek culture doomed to be to that extent one-sided. It will, we may hope, be the great triumph of the modern love (when it becomes more of a true comradeship between man and woman than it yet is) to give both to society and to the individual the grandest inspirations, and perhaps in conjunction with the other attachment, to lift the modern nations to a higher level of political and artistic advancement than even the Greeks attained. I quote one or two modern writers on the subject, and then some passages from Plato and others indicating the philosophy of friendship as entertained among the Greeks.

Place of Friendship

Place of Friendship

B ISHOP THIRLWALL, that excellent thinker and scholar, in his *History of Greece* (vol. 1, p. 176) says:—

Bishop Thirlwall on Greek Friendship

"O NE of the noblest and most amiable sides of the Greek character is the readiness with which it lent itself to construct intimate and durable friendships; and this is a feature no less prominent in the earliest than in the latest times. It was indeed connected with the comparatively low estimation in which female society was held; but the devotedness and constancy with which these attachments were maintained was not the less admirable and engaging. The heroic companions whom we find celebrated, partly by Homer and partly in traditions, which if not of equal antiquity were grounded on the same feeling, seem to have but one heart and soul, with scarcely a wish or object apart, and only to live, as they are always ready to die, for one another. It is true that the relation between them is not always one of perfect equality: but this is a circumstance which, while it often adds a peculiar charm to the poetical description, detracts little from the dignity of the idea which it presents. Such were the friendships of Hercules and Ioläus, of Theseus and Pirithöus, of Orestes and Pylades: and though these may owe

44

the greater part of their fame to the later epic or even dramatic poetry, the moral groundwork undoubtedly subsisted in the period to which the tradition referred. The argument of the Iliad mainly turns on the affection of Achilles for Patroclus—whose love for the greater hero is only tempered by reverence for his higher birth and his unequalled prowess. But the mutual regard which united Idomeneus and Meriones, Diomedes and Sthenelus—though, as the persons themselves are less important, it is kept more in the background—is manifestly viewed by the poet in the same light. The idea of a Greek hero seems not to have been thought complete, without such a brother in arms by his side."

The following is from Ludwig Frey (*Der Eros und die Kunst*, p. 33):—

"LET it then be repeated: love for a youth was *Compared* for the Greeks something sacred, and can on- *to* ly be compared with our German homage to *Chivalry* women—say the chivalric love of mediæval times."

LOWES DICKINSON, in his *Greek View of Life*, noting the absence of romance in the relations between men and women of that civilisation, says:

45

"NEVERTHELESS, it would be a mistake to conclude, from these conditions, that the element of romance was absent from Greek life. The fact is simply that with them it took a different form, that of passionate friendship between men. Such friendships, of course, occur in all nations and at all times, but among the Greeks they were, we might say, an institution. Their ideal was the development and education of the younger by the older man, and in this view they were recognised and approved by custom and law as an important factor in the state." *Greek View of Life*, p. 167.

"SO much indeed were the Greeks impressed with the manliness of this passion, with its power to prompt to high thought and heroic action, that some of the best of them set the love of man for man far above that of man for woman. The one, they maintained, was primarily of the spirit, the other primarily of the flesh; the one bent upon shaping to the type of all manly excellence both the body and the soul of the beloved, the other upon a passing pleasure of the senses." *Ibid*, p. 172.

The following are some remarks of J. A. Symonds on the same subject :—

"PARTLY owing to the social habits of their cities, and partly to the peculiar notions which

46

they entertained regarding the seclusion of free *Relation to* women in the home, all the higher elements of *Women* spiritual and mental activity, and the conditions under which a generous passion was conceivable, had become the exclusive privileges of men. It was not that women occupied a semi-servile station, as some students have imagined, or that within the sphere of the household they were not the respected and trusted helpmates of men.   But circumstances rendered it impossible for them to excite romantic and enthusiastic passion. The exaltation of the emotions was reserved for the male sex." *A Problem in Greek Ethics*, p. 68.

And he continues :—

"SOCRATES therefore sought to direct and *J. A.* moralise a force already existing. In the *Phædrus Symonds* he describes the passion of love between man and *on Socrates* boy as a '*mania*,' not different in quality from that which inspires poets ; and after painting that fervid picture of the lover, he declares that the true object of a noble life can only be attained by passionate friends, bound together in the chains of close yet temperate comradeship, seeking always to advance in knowledge, self-restraint, and intellectual illumination. The doctrine of the *Symposium* is not different, except that Socrates here takes a higher

47

flight. The same love is treated as the method whereby the soul may begin her mystic journey to the region of essential beauty, truth, and goodness. It has frequently been remarked that Plato's dialogues have to be read as poems even more than as philosophical treatises; and if this be true at all, it is particularly true of both the *Phædrus* and the *Symposium*. The lesson which both essays seem intended to inculcate, is this: love, like poetry and prophecy, is a divine gift, which diverts men from the common current of their lives; but in the right use of this gift lies the secret of all human excellence. The passion which grovels in the filth of sensual grossness may be transformed into a glorious en-enthusiasm, a winged splendour, capable of soaring to the contemplation of eternal verities."

ON the *Symposium* or *Banquet* of Plato (B.C. 428—B.C. 347), a supper party is supposed, at which a discussion on love and friendship takes place. The friends present speak in turn—the enthusiastic Phædrus, the clear-headed Pausanias, the grave doctor Eryximachus, the comic and acute Aristophanes, the young poet Agathon; Socrates, tantalising, suggestive, and quoting the profound sayings of the

48

prophetess Diotima; and Alcibiades, drunk, and quite ready to drink more;—each in his turn, out of the fulness of his heart, speaks; and thus in this most dramatic dialogue we have love discussed from every point of view, and with insight, acumen, romance and humour unrivalled.

Phædrus and Pausanias, in the two following quotations, take the line which perhaps most thoroughly represents the public opinion of the day—as to the value of friendship in nurturing a spirit of honour and freedom, especially in matters military and political:—

"THUS numerous are the witnesses who acknowledge love to be the eldest of the gods. And not only is he the eldest, he is also the source of the greatest benefits to us. For I know not any greater blessing to a young man beginning life than a virtuous lover, or to the lover than a beloved youth. For the principle which ought to be the guide of men who would nobly live—that principle, I say, neither kindred, nor honour, nor wealth, nor any other motive is able to implant so well as love. Of what am I speaking? of the sense of honour and dishonour, without which neither

From the Speech of Phædrus in the Symposium

49   𝖆 SHEET FIVE

states nor individuals ever do any good or great work. And I say that a lover who is detected in doing any dishonorable act, or submitting through cowardice when any dishonour is done to him by another, will be more pained at being detected by his beloved than at being seen by his father, or by his companions, or by anyone else. The beloved too, when he is seen in any disgraceful situation, has the same feeling about his lover. And if there were only some way of contriving that a state or an army should be made up of lovers and their loves, they would be the very best governors of their own city, abstaining from all dishonour, and emulating one another in honour; and when fighting at one another's side, although a mere handful, they would overcome the world. For what lover would not choose rather to be seen by all mankind than by his beloved, either when abandoning his post or throwing away his arms? He would be ready to die a thousand deaths rather than endure this. Or who would desert his beloved, or fail him in the hour of danger? The veriest coward would become an inspired hero, equal to the bravest, at such a time; love would inspire him. That courage which, as Homer says, the god breathes into the soul of heroes, love of his own nature infuses into the lover." *Symposium of Plato, trans. B. Jowett.*

"IN Ionia and other places, and generally in countries which are subject to the barbarians, the custom is held to be dishonorable; loves of youths share the evil repute of philosophy and gymnastics, because they are inimical to tyranny; for the interests of rulers require that their subjects should be poor in spirit, and that there should be no strong bond of friendship or society among them, which love above all other motives is likely to inspire, as our Athenian tyrants learned by experience." *Ibid.*

ARISTOPHANES goes more deeply into the nature of this love of which they are speaking. He says it is a profound reality—a deep and intimate union, abiding after death, and making of the lovers "one departed soul instead of two." But in order to explain his allusion to "the other half" it must be premised that in the earlier part of his speech he has in a serio-comic vein pretended that human beings were originally constructed double, with four legs, four arms, etc.; but that as a punishment for their sins Zeus divided them perpendicularly, "as folk cut eggs before they salt them," the males into

two parts, the females into two, and the hermaphro-
dites likewise into two—since when, these divided
people have ever pursued their lost halves, and
"thrown their arms around and embraced each
other, seeking to grow together again." And so,
speaking of those who were originally males, he says:

' A ND these when they grow up are our statesmen, and these only, which is a great proof of
the truth of what I am saying. And when they reach
manhood they are lovers of youth, and are not
naturally inclined to marry or beget children, which
they do, if at all, only in obedience to the law, but
they are satisfied if they may be allowed to live with
one another unwedded; and such a nature is prone
to love and ready to return love, always embracing
that which is akin to him. And when one of them
finds his other half, whether he be a lover of youth
or a lover of another sort, the pair are lost in an
amazement of love and friendship and intimacy,
and one will not be out of the other's sight, as I may
say, even for a moment: they will pass their whole
lives together; yet they could not explain what
they desire of one another. For the intense yearning that each of them has towards the other does
not appear to be the desire of lovers' intercourse,

but of something else which the soul of either evidently desires and cannot tell, and of which she only has a dark and doubtful presentiment. Suppose Hephæstus, with his instruments, to come to the pair who are lying side by side and say to them, 'What do you people want of one another?' they would be unable to explain. And suppose further that when he saw their perplexity he said : 'Do you desire to be wholly one ; always day and night to be in one another's company? for if this is what you desire, I am ready to melt you into one and let you grow together, so that being two you shall become one, and while you live, live a common life as if you were a single man, and after your death in the world below still be one departed soul instead of two—I ask whether this is what you lovingly desire, and whether you are satisfied to attain this?'— there is not a man of them who when he heard the proposal would deny or would not acknowledge that this meeting and melting in one another's arms, this becoming one instead of two, was the very expression of his ancient need." *Ibid.*

SOCRATES, in his speech, and especially in the later portion of it where he quotes his supposed tutoress Diotima, carries the argument up to its highest issue. After contending for the essentially creative, generative nature of love, not only in the Body but in the Soul, he proceeds to say that it is not so much the seeking of a lost half which causes the creative impulse in lovers, as the fact that in our mortal friends we are contemplating (though unconsciously) an image of the Essential and Divine Beauty; it is this that affects us with that wonderful "mania," and lifts us into the region where we become creators. And he follows on to the conclusion that it is by wisely and truly loving our visible friends that at last, after long long experience, there dawns upon us the vision of that Absolute Beauty which by mortal eyes must ever remain unseen:—

Speech of Socrates "HE who has been instructed thus far in the things of love, and who has learned to see the beautiful in due order and succession, when he comes towards the end will suddenly perceive a nature of wondrous beauty . . . . beauty absolute, separate, simple and everlasting, which without diminution and without increase, or any change, is imparted to the evergrowing and perishing beauties of all other things. He who, from these ascen-

54

ding under the influence of true love, begins to perceive that beauty, is not far from the end." *Ibid*.

This is indeed the culmination, for Plato, of all existence—the ascent into the presence of that endless Beauty of which all fair mortal things are but the mirrors. But to condense this great speech of Socrates is impossible; only to persistent and careful reading (if even then) will it yield up all its treasures.

IN the dialogue named *Phædrus* the same idea is worked out, only to some extent in reverse order. As in the *Symposium* the lover by rightly loving at last rises to the vision of the Supreme Beauty; so in the *Phædrus* it is explained that in reality every soul *has* at some time seen that Vision (at the time, namely, of its true initiation, when it was indeed winged)—but has forgotten it; and that it is the dim *reminiscence* of that Vision, constantly working within us, which guides us to our earthly loves and renders their effect upon us so transporting. Long ago, in some other condition of being, we saw Beauty herself:—

Place of Friendship

BUT of beauty, I repeat again that we saw her
there shining in company with the celestial
forms; and coming to earth we find her here too,
shining in clearness through the clearest aperture
of sense. For sight is the keenest of our bodily senses; though not by that is wisdom seen; her loveliness would have been transporting if there had
been a visible image of her, and the same is true of
the loveliness of the other ideas as well. But this is
the privilege of beauty, that she is the loveliest and
also the most palpable to sight. Now he who is not
newly initiated, or who has become corrupted, does
not easily rise out of this world to the sight of
true beauty in the other; he looks only at her
earthly namesake, and instead of being awed at the
sight of her, like a brutish beast he rushes on to
enjoy and beget; he consorts with wantonness, and
is not afraid or ashamed of pursuing pleasure in
violation of nature. But he whose initiation is re-
cent, and who has been the spectator of many
glories in the other world, is amazed when he sees
anyone having a god-like face or form, which is the
expression of Divine Beauty; and at first a shudder
runs through him, and again the old awe steals
over him; then looking upon the face of his beloved as of a god he reverences him, and if he were
not afraid of being thought a downright madman,

he would sacrifice to his beloved as to the image of a god." *The Phædrus of Plato, trans. B. Jowett.*

And again :—

'AND so the beloved who, like a god, has received every true and loyal service from his lover, not in pretence but in reality, being also himself of a nature friendly to his admirer, if in former days he has blushed to own his passion and turned away his lover, because his youthful companions or others slanderously told him that he would be disgraced, now as years advance, at the appointed age and time, is led to receive him into communion. For fate which has ordained that there shall be no friendship among the evil has also ordained that there shall ever be friendship among the good. And when he has received him into communion and intimacy, then the beloved is amazed at the goodwill of the lover; he recognises that the inspired friend is worth all other friendships or kinships, which have nothing of friendship in them in comparison. And when this feeling continues and he is nearer to him and embraces him, in gymnastic exercises and at other times of meeting, then does the fountain of that stream, which Zeus when he was in love with Ganymede named desire, overflow upon the lover, and some enters into his soul, and some when he is filled flows out again; and as a breeze or an echo rebounds from the smooth rocks and returns whence it came, so does the stream of beauty, passing the eyes which are the natural doors and windows of the soul, re-turn again to the beautiful one; there arriving and quickening the passages of the wings, watering them and inclining them to grow, and filling the soul of the beloved also with love." *Ibid.*

For Plato the real power which ever moves the soul is this reminiscence of the Beauty which exists before all worlds. In the actual world the soul lives but in anguish, an exile from her true home; but in the presence of her friend, who reveals the Divine, she is loosed from her suffering and comes to her haven of rest.

Socrates in the Phædrus "AND wherever she [the soul] thinks that she will behold the beautiful one, thither in her desire she runs. And when she has seen him, and bathed herself with the waters of desire, her con-straint is loosened, and she is refreshed, and has no more pangs and pains; and this is the sweetest of all pleasures at the time, and is the reason why the soul of the lover will never forsake his beautiful one, whom he esteems above all; he has forgotten mother and brethren and companions, and he thinks nothing of the neglect and loss of his property; the rules and proprieties of life, on which he formerly prided himself, he now despises, and is ready to sleep like a servant, wherever he is allowed, as near as he can to his beautiful one, who is not only the object of his worship, but the only physician who can heal him in his extreme agony." *Ibid.*

AT another time, in the Banquet of Xenophon, Socrates is again made to speak at length on the subject of Love—though not in so inspired a strain as in Plato :—

"TRULY, to speak for one, I never remember the time when I was not in love; I know too that Charmides has had a great many lovers, and being much beloved has loved again. As for Critobulus, he is still of an age to love, and to be beloved; and Nicerates too, who loves so passionately his wife, at least as report goes, is equally beloved by her. . . . And as for you, Callias, you love, as well as the rest of us; for who is it that is ignorant of your love for Autolycus? It is the town-talk; and foreigners, as well as our citizens, are *The Banquet of Xenophon*

59

acquainted with it. The reason for your loving him, I believe to be that you are both born of illustrious families; and at the same time are both possessed of personal qualities that render you yet more illustrious. For me, I always admired the sweetness and evenness of your temper; but much more when I consider that your passion for Autolycus is placed on a person who has nothing luxurious or affected in him; but in all things shows a vigour and temperance worthy of a virtuous soul; which is a proof at the same time that if he is infinitely beloved, he deserves to be so. I confess indeed I am not firmly persuaded whether there be but one Venus or two, the celestial and the vulgar; and it may be with this goddess, as with Jupiter, who has many different names though there is still but one Jupiter. But I know very well that both the Venuses have quite different altars, temples and sacrifices. The vulgar Venus is worshipped after a common negligent manner; whereas the celestial one is adored in purity and sanctity of life. The vulgar inspires mankind with the love of the body only, but the celestial fires the mind with the love of the soul, with friendship, and a generous thirst after noble actions. . . . Nor is it hard to prove, Callias, that gods and heroes have always had more passion and esteem for the charms of the soul, than those of the body: at least this seems to have been the opinion of our ancient authors. For we may observe in the fables of antiquity that Jupiter, who loved several mortals on account of their personal beauty only, never conferred upon them immortality. Whereas it was otherwise with Hercules, Castor, Pollux, and several others; for having admired and applauded the greatness of their courage and the beauty of their minds, he enrolled them in the number of the gods. . . . You are then infinitely obliged to the gods, Callias, who have inspired you with love and friendship for Autolycus, as they have inspired Critobulus with the same for Amandra; for real and pure friendship knows no difference in sexes." *Banquet of Xenophon* § viii. *(Boh)*.

PLUTARCH, who wrote in the first century A.D. (nearly 500 years after Plato), carried on the tradition of his master, though with an admixture of later influences; and philosophised about friendship, on the basis of true love being a reminiscence.

"THE rainbow is I suppose a reflection caused by the sun's rays falling on a moist cloud, making us think the appearance is in the cloud.

Place of Friendship

Similarly erotic fancy in the case of noble souls causes a reflection of the memory from things which here appear and are called beautiful to what is really divine and lovely and felicitous and wonderful. But most lovers pursuing and groping after the semblance of beauty in youths and women, as in mirrors,[a] can derive nothing more certain than pleasure mixed with pain. And this seems the love-delirium of Ixion, who instead of the joy he desired embraced only a cloud, as children who desire to take the rainbow into their hands, clutching at whatever they see. But different is the behaviour of the noble and chaste lover: for he reflects on the divine beauty that can only be felt, while he uses the beauty of the visible body only as an organ of the memory, though he embraces it and loves it, and associating with it is still more inflamed in mind. And so neither in the body do they sit ever gazing at and desiring *this* light, nor after death do they return to this world again, and skulk and loiter about the doors and bedchambers of newly-married people, disagreeable ghosts of pleasure-loving and sensual men and women, who do not rightly deserve the name of

[a] "For now we see by means of a mirror darkly (lit. enigmatically); but then face to face; now I know in part; but then shall I know even as also I am known." 1 *Cor.* xiii. 12.

lovers. For the true lover, when he has got into the other world and associated with beauties as much as is lawful, has wings and is initiated and passes his time above in the presence of his Deity, dancing and waiting upon him, until he goes back to the meadows of the Moon and Aphrodite, and sleeping there commences a new existence. But this is a subject too high for the present occasion."
Plutarch's Eroticus § xx. *trans. Bohn's Classics.*

III.

Poetry of Friendship among Greeks & Romans

Poetry of Friendship
among Greeks & Romans

THE fact, already mentioned, that the *romance* of love among the Greeks was chiefly felt towards male friends, naturally led to their poetry being largely inspired by friendship; and Greek literature contains such a great number of poems of this sort, that I have thought it worth while to dedicate the main portion of the following section to quotations from them. No translations of course can do justice to the beauty of the originals, but the few specimens given may help to illustrate the depth and tenderness as well as the temperance and sobriety which on the whole characterised Greek feeling on this subject, at any rate during the best period of Hellenic culture. The remainder of the section is devoted to Roman poetry of the time of the Cæsars.

Poetry of Friendship

It is not always realised that the Iliad of Homer turns upon the motive of friendship, but the extracts immediately following will perhaps make this clear. E. F. M. Benecke in his *Position of Women in Greek Poetry* (p. 76) says of the Iliad :—

Motive of Homer's Iliad

"IT is a story of which the main motive is the love of Achilles for Patroclus. This solution is astoundingly simple, and yet it took me so long to bring myself to accept it that I am quite ready to forgive anyone who feels a similar hesitation. But those who do accept it cannot fail to observe, on further consideration, how thoroughly suitable a motive of this kind would be in a national Greek epic. For this is the motive running through the whole of Greek life, till that life was transmuted by the influence of Macedonia. The lover-warriors Achilles and Patroclus are the direct spiritual ancestors of the sacred Band of Thebans, who died to a man on the field of Chæronæa."

The following two quotations are from *The Greek Poets* by J. A. Symonds, ch. iii. p. 80 *et seq.* :—

"THE *Iliad* therefore has for its whole subject the passion of Achilles—that ardent energy or μῆνις of the hero which displayed itself first as anger against Agamemnon, and afterwards as love

68

for the lost Patroclus. The truth of this was per- *J. A. Symonds on the same*
ceived by one of the greatest poets and profoundest
critics of the modern world, Dante. When Dante,
in the *Inferno*, wished to describe Achilles, he
wrote, with characteristic brevity :—

> "Achille
> Che per amore al fine combatteo."
> ("Achilles
> Who at the last was brought to fight by love.")

"In this pregnant sentence Dante sounded the
whole depth of the *Iliad*. The wrath of Achilles for
Agamemnon, which prevented him at first from
fighting; the love of Achilles, passing the love of
women, for Patroclus, which induced him to fore-
go his anger and to fight at last; these are the two
poles on which the *Iliad* turns."

After his quarrel with Agamemnon, not even all
the losses of the Greeks and the entreaties of Agamemnon himself will induce Achilles to fight—not
till Patroclus is slain by Hector—Patroclus, his dear
friend "whom above all my comrades I honoured,
even as myself." Then he rises up, dons his armour,
and driving the Trojans before him revenges himself on the body of Hector. But Patroclus lies yet

unburied; and when the fighting is over, to Achilles comes the ghost of his dead friend:—

Achilles and Patroclus

"THE son of Peleus, by the shore of the roaring sea lay, heavily groaning, surrounded by his Myrmidons; on a fair space of sand he lay, where the waves lapped the beach. Then slumber took him, loosing the cares of his heart, and mantling softly around him, for sorely wearied were his radiant limbs with driving Hector on by windy Troy. There to him came the soul of poor Patroclus, in all things like himself, in stature, and in the beauty of his eyes and voice, and on the form was raiment like his own. He stood above the hero's head, and spake to him:—

"'Sleepest thou, and me hast thou forgotten, Achilles? Not in my life wert thou neglectful of me, but in death. Bury me soon, that I may pass the gates of Hades. Far off the souls, the shadows of the dead, repel me, nor suffer me to join them on the river bank; but, as it is, thus I roam around the wide-doored house of Hades. But stretch to me thy hand I entreat; for never again shall I return from Hades when once ye shall have given me the meed of funeral fire. Nay, never shall we sit in life apart from our dear comrades and take counsel together. But me hath hateful fate enveloped—fate that was mine at the moment of my birth. And for thyself, divine Achilles, it is doomed to die beneath the noble Trojan's wall. Another thing I say to thee, and bid thee do it if thou wilt obey me:—lay not my bones apart from thine, Achilles, but lay them together; for we were brought up together in your house, when Menœtius brought me, a child, from Opus to your house, because of woeful bloodshed on the day in which I slew the son of Amphidamas, myself a child, not willing it but in anger at our games. Then did the horseman, Peleus, take me, and rear me in his house, and cause me to be called thy squire. So then let one grave also hide the bones of both of us, the golden urn thy goddess-mother gave to thee.'

"Him answered swift-footed Achilles:—

'Why, dearest and most honoured, hast thou hither come, to lay on me this thy behest? All things most certainly will I perform, and bow to what thou biddest. But stand thou near: even for one moment let us throw our arms upon each other's neck, and take our fill of sorrowful wailing.'

"So spake he, and with his outstretched hands he clasped, but could not seize. The spirit, earthward, like smoke, vanished with a shriek. Then all astonished arose Achilles, and beat his palms together, and spake a piteous word:—

71

'Heavens! is there then, among the dead, soul and the shade of life, but thought is theirs no more at all? For through the night the soul of poor Patroclus stood above my head, wailing and sorrowing loud, and bade me do his will; it was the very semblance of himself.'

"So spake he, and in the hearts of all of them he raised desire of lamentation; and while they were yet mourning, to them appeared rose-fingered dawn about the piteous corpse." *Iliad*, xxiii. 59 *et seq.*

Plato on the above

PLATO in the *Symposium* dwells tenderly on this relation between Achilles and Patroclus:—

[AND great] "was the reward of the true love of Achilles towards his lover Patroclus—his lover and not his love (the notion that Patroclus was the beloved one is a foolish error into which Æschylus has fallen, for Achilles was surely the fairer of the two, fairer also than all the other heroes; and, as Homer informs us, he was still beardless, and younger far). And greatly as the gods honour the virtue of love, still the return of love on the part of the beloved to the lover is more admired and valued and rewarded by them, for the lover has a nature more divine and worthy of worship. Now Achilles was quite aware, for he had been told by his mother, that he might avoid death and return home, and live to a good old age, if he abstained from slaying Hector. Nevertheless he gave his life to revenge his friend, and dared to die, not only on his behalf, but after his death. Wherefore the gods honoured him even above Alcestis, and sent him to the Islands of the Blest." *Symposium, speech of Phædrus, trans. by B. Jowett.*

And on this passage Symonds has the following note :—

"PLATO, discussing the *Myrmidones* of Æs- *Criticism* chylus, remarks in the *Symposium* that the *of Plato's* tragic poet was wrong to make Achilles the lover *View* of Patroclus, seeing that Patroclus was the elder of the two, and that Achilles was the youngest and most beautiful of all the Greeks. The fact however is that Homer raises no question in our minds about the relation of lover and beloved. Achilles and Patroclus are comrades. Their friendship is equal. It was only the reflective activity of the Greek mind, working upon the Homeric legend by the light of subsequent custom, which introduced these distinctions." *The Greek Poets*, ch. iii. p. 103.

From the time of Homer onwards, Greek literature was full of songs celebrating friendship:—

Athenæus "AND in fact there was such emulation about composing poems of this sort, and so far was any one from thinking lightly of the amatory poets, that Æschylus, who was a very great poet, and Sophocles too introduced the subject of the loves of men on the stage in their tragedies: the one describing the love of Achilles for Patroclus, and the other, in his Niobe, the mutual love of her sons (on which account some have given an ill name to that tragedy); and all such passages as those are very agreeable to the spectators." *Athenæus*, bk. xiii. ch. 75.

ONE of the earlier Greek poets was Theognis (B.C. 550) whose Gnomæ or Maxims were a series of verses mostly addressed to his young friend Kurnus, whom by this means he sought to guide and instruct out of the stores of his own riper experience. The verses are reserved and didactic for the most part, but now and then, as in the following passage, show deep underlying feeling:—

74

Greeks & Romans

"LO, I have given thee wings wherewith to fly *From*
    Over the boundless ocean and the earth;   *Theognis*
Yea, on the lips of many shalt thou lie
    The comrade of their banquet and their mirth.
Youths in their loveliness shall make thee sound
    Upon the silver flute's melodious breath;
And when thou goest darkling underground
    Down to the lamentable house of death,
Oh yet not then from honour shalt thou cease,
    But wander, an imperishable name,
Kurnus, about the seas and shores of Greece,
    Crossing from isle to isle the barren main.
Horses thou shalt not need, but lightly ride
    Sped by the Muses of the violet crown,
And men to come, while earth and sun abide,
    Who cherish song shall cherish thy renown.
Yea, I have given thee wings! and in return
    Thou givest me the scorn with which I burn."

Theognis Gnomai, lines 237-254,
trans. by G. Lowes Dickinson.

AS Theognis had his well-loved disciples, so had the poetess Sappho (600 B.C.) Her devotion to her girl-friends and companions is indeed proverbial.

75

Sappho "WHAT Alcibiades and Charmides and Phædrus were to Socrates, Gyrinna and Atthis and Anactoria were to the Lesbian." *Max Tyrius, quoted in H. T. Wharton's Sappho*, p. 23.

Perhaps the few lines of Sappho, translated or paraphrased by Catullus under the title *To Lesbia*, form the most celebrated fragment of her extant work. They may be roughly rendered thus:—

To Lesbia "PEER of all the gods unto me appeareth
He of men who sitting beside thee heareth
Close at hand thy syllabled words sweet spoken,
   Or loving laughter—

That sweet laugh which flutters my heart and bosom.
For, at sight of thee, in an instant fail me
Voice and speech, and under my skin there courses
   Swiftly a thin flame;

Darkness is on my eyes, in my ears a drumming,
Drenched in sweat my frame, my body trembling;
Paler ev'n than grass—'tis, I doubt, but little
   From death divides me."

Greeks & Romans

SEVERAL of the odes of Anacreon (B.C. 520) are addressed to his young friend Bathyllus. The following short one has been preserved to us by Athenæus (bk. xiii. § 17):—

> "O BOY, with virgin-glancing eye,
>   I call thee, but thou dost not hear;
> Thou know'st not how my soul doth cry
>   For thee, its charioteer."

Anacreon to Bathyllus

Anacreon had not the passion and depth of Sappho, but there is a mark of genuine feeling in some of his poems, as in this simple little epigram:—

> "ON their hindquarters horses
>   Are branded oft with fire,
> And anyone knows a Parthian
>   Because he wears a tiar;
> And I at sight of lovers
>   Their nature can declare,
> For in their hearts they too
>   Some subtle flame-mark bear."

Epigram on Lovers

The following fragment is from Pindar's Ode to his young friend Theoxenos—in whose arms Pindar is said to have died (B.C. 442):—

Pindar to Theoxenos

"O SOUL, 'tis thine in season meet,
　　To pluck of love the blossom sweet,
When hearts are young:
But he who sees the blazing beams,
The light that from *that* forehead streams,
　　And is not stung;—
Who is not storm-tossed with desire,—
Lo! he, I ween, with frozen fire,
Of adamant or stubborn steel
Is forged in his cold heart that cannot feel."

*Trans. by J. Addington Symonds,
The Greek Poets*, vol. 1, p. 286.

PLATO'S epigrams on Aster and Agathon are well known. The two first-quoted make a play of course on the name Aster (star).

To Aster:

Epigrams of Plato

"THOU wert the morning star among the living,
　　Ere thy fair light had fled;
Now, having died, thou art as Hesperus, giving
　　New splendour to the dead."

(Shelley.)

Greeks & Romans

To the same:

"THOU at the stars dost gaze, who art *my* star
    —O would that I were
Heaven, to gaze on thee, ever with thousands of
    eyes."

To Agathon:

"THEE as I kist, behold! on my lips my own
    soul was trembling;
For, bold one, she had come, meaning to find her
    way through."

There are many other epigrams and songs on the
same subject from the Greek writers. The following
is by Meleager (a native of Gadara in Palestine)
about 60 B.C., and one of the sweetest and most
human of the lyric poets :—

"O MORTALS crossed in love! the Southwind, *Meleager*
    see!
That blows so fair for sailor folk, hath ta'en
Half of my soul, Andragathos, from me.
    Thrice happy ships, thrice blessèd billowy main,
And four times favored wind that bears the youth,
O would I were a Dolphin! so, in truth,
High on my shoulders ferried he should come
To Rhodes, sweet haunt of boys, his island-home."

From the Greek Anthology, ii. 402.

79

Also from the Greek Anthology:—

Epigram "O SAY, and again repeat, fair, fair—and still
I will say it—
How fair, my friend, and good to see, thou art;
On pine or oak or wall thy name I do not blazon—
Love has too deeply graved it in my heart."

"PERHAPS the most beautiful [says J. A. Sy-
monds] of the sepulchral epigrams is one by
an unknown writer, of which I here give a free
paraphrase. *Anth. Pal.*, vii. 346:—

Epitaph
Anonymous

'Of our great love, Parthenophil,
This little stone abideth still
 Sole sign and token:
I seek thee yet, and yet shall seek,
Tho' faint mine eyes, my spirit weak
 With prayers unspoken.

Meanwhile best friend of friends, do thou,
If this the cruel fates allow,
 By death's dark river,
Among those shadowy people, drink
No drop for me on Lethe's brink:
 Forget me never!'"

The Greek Poets, vol. 2, p. 298.

Greeks & Romans

THEOCRITUS, though coming late in the Greek age (about 300 B.C.) when Athens had yielded place to Alexandria, still carried on the Greek tradition in a remarkable way. A native of Syracuse, he caught and echoed in a finer form the life and songs of the country folk of that region—themselves descendants of Dorian settlers. Songs and ballads full of similar notes linger among the Greek peasants, shepherds and fisher-folk, even down to the present day.

The following poem (trans. by M. J. Chapman, 1836) is one of the best known and most beautiful of his Idyls:—

Idyl XII.

"ART come, dear youth? two days and nights *Theocritus*
    away!   *Idyl XII.*
(Who burn with love, grow aged in a day.)
As much as apples sweet the damson crude
Excel; the blooming spring the winter rude;
In fleece the sheep her lamb; the maid in sweetness
The thrice-wed dame; the fawn the calf in fleet-
    ness;

◢ SHEET SEVEN

The nightingale in song all feathered kind—
So much thy longed-for presence cheers my mind
To thee I hasten, as to shady beech,
The traveller, when from the heaven's reach
The sun fierce blazes. May our love be strong,
To all hereafter times the theme of song!
'Two men each other loved to that degree,
That either friend did in the other see
A dearer than himself. They lived of old
Both golden natures in an age of gold.'

O father Zeus! ageless immortals all!
Two hundred ages hence may one recall,
Down-coming to the irremeable river,
This to my mind, and this good news deliver:
'E'en now from east to west, from north to south,
Your mutual friendship lives in every mouth.'
This, as they please, th' Olympians will decide:
Of thee, by blooming virtue beautified,
My glowing song shall only truth disclose;
With falsehood's pustules I'll not shame my nose.
If thou dost sometime grieve me, sweet the plea-
  sure
Of reconcilement, joy in double measure
To find thou never didst intend the pain,
And feel myself from all doubt free again.

And ye Megarians, at Nisæa dwelling,
Expert at rowing, mariners excelling,
Be happy ever! for with honours due
Th' Athenian Diocles, to friendship true
Ye celebrate. With the first blush of spring
The youth surround his tomb: there who shall
    bring
The sweetest kiss, whose lip is purest found,
Back to his mother goes with garlands crowned.
Nice touch the arbiter must have indeed,
And must, methinks, the blue-eyed Ganymede
Invoke with many prayers—a mouth to own
True to the touch of lips, as Lydian stone
To proof of gold—which test will instant show
The pure or base, as money changers know."

The following Idyl, of which I append a render-
ing, is attributed to Theocritus:—

Idyl XXIX.

"THEY say, dear boy, that wine and truth agree;
    And, being in wine, I'll tell the truth to thee—
Yes, all that works in secret in my soul.
'Tis this: thou dost not love me with thy whole
Untampered heart. I know; for half my time
Is spent in gazing on thy beauty's prime;

Idyl The other half is nought. When thou art good,
XXIX. My days are like the gods'; but when the mood
Tormenting takes thee, 'tis my night of woe.
How were it right to vex a lover so?
Take my advice, my lad, thine elder friend,
'Twill make thee glad and grateful in the end:
In one tree build one nest, so no grim snake
May creep upon thee. For to-day thou'lt make
Thy home on one branch, and to-morrow changing
Wilt seek another, to what's new still ranging;
And should a stranger praise your handsome face,
Him more than three-year-proven friend you'll
    grace,
While him who loved you first you'll treat as cold
As some acquaintanceship of three days old.
Thou fliest high, methinks, in love and pride;
But I would say: keep ever at thy side
A mate that is thine equal; doing so,
The townsfolk shall speak well of thee alway,
And love shall never visit thee with woe—
Love that so easily men's hearts can flay,
And mine has conquered that was erst of steel.
Nay, by thy gracious lips I make appeal:
Remember thou wert younger a year agone
And we grow grey and wrinkled, all, or e'er
We can escape our doom; of mortals none
His youth retakes again, for azure wings

84

Are on her shoulders, and we sons of care
Are all too slow to catch such flying things.

Mindful of this, be gentle, is my prayer,
And love me, guileless, ev'n as I love thee;
So when thou hast a beard, such friends as were
Achilles and Patroclus we may be."

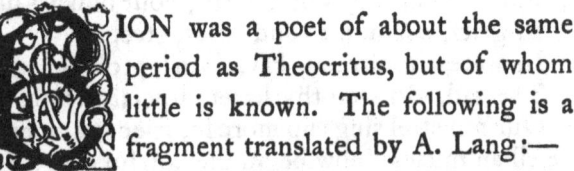ION was a poet of about the same period as Theocritus, but of whom little is known. The following is a fragment translated by A. Lang:—

"HAPPY are they that love, when with equal *Bion* love they are rewarded. Happy was Theseus, when Pirithous was by his side, yea tho' he went down to the house of implacable Hades. Happy among hard men and inhospitable was Orestes, for that Pylades chose to share his wanderings. And *he* was happy, Achilles Æacides, while his darling lived,—happy was he in his death, because he avenged the dread fate of Patroclus." *Theocritus, Bion and Moschus, Golden Treasury series,* p. 182.

The beautiful *Lament for Bion* by Moschus is interesting in this connection, and should be com-

85

pared with Shelley's lament for Keats in *Adonais*—
for which latter poem indeed it supplied some
suggestions :—

Lament "YE mountain valleys, pitifully groan!
for Bion Rivers and Dorian springs for Bion weep!
by Ye plants drop tears! ye groves lamenting moan!
Moschus Exhale your life, wan flowers; your blushes deep
 In grief, anemonies and roses, steep!
 In softest murmurs, Hyacinth! prolong
 The sad, sad woe thy lettered petals keep;
 Our minstrel sings no more his friends among
Sicilian muses! now begin the doleful song."

*M. J. Chapman trans. in the
Greek Pastoral Poets,* 1836.

The allusion to Hyacinth is thus explained by
Chapman :—

Story "HYACINTHUS, a Spartan youth, the son
of Hya- of Clio, was in great favour with Apollo.
cinthus Zephyrus, being enraged that he preferred Apollo to him, blew the discus when flung by
Apollo, on a day that Hyacinthus was playing at
discus-throwing with that god, against the head
of the youth, and so killed him. Apollo, being

unable to save his life, changed him into the flower which was named after him, and on whose petals the Greeks fancied they could trace the notes of grief, ἀι, ἀι.^a A festival called the Hyacinthia was celebrated for three days in each year at Sparta, in honour of the god and his unhappy favorite." *Note to Moschus*, Idyl iii.

^aSeen within the flower we call Larkspur

The story of Apollo and Hyacinth is gracefully told by Ovid, in the tenth book of his Metamorphoses :—

"MIDWAY betwixt the past and coming night
   Stood Titan^a when the pair, their limbs un-
     robed,
And glist'ning with the olive's unctuous juice,
In friendly contest with the discus vied."

Told by Ovid

^aThe Sun

[The younger one is struck by the discus ; and like a fading flower]

"To its own weight unequal drooped the head
Of Hyacinth ; and o'er him wailed the god :—
Liest thou so, Œbalia's child, of youth
Untimely robbed, and wounded by my fault—
At once my grief and guilt ?—This hand hath dealt

87

Thy death! 'Tis I who send thee to the grave!
And yet scarce guilty, unless guilt it were
To sport, or guilt to love thee! Would this life
Might thine redeem, or be with thine resigned!
But thou—since Fate denies a god to die—
Be present with me ever! Let thy name
Dwell ever in my heart and on my lips,
Theme of my lyre and burden of my song;
And ever bear the echo of my wail
Writ on thy new-born flower! The time shall come
When, with thyself associate, to its name
The mightiest of the Greeks shall link his own.
   Prophetic as Apollo mourned, the blood
That with its dripping crimson dyed the turf
Was blood no more: and sudden sprang to life
A flower."

Ovid's Metamorphoses trans.
H. King, London, 1871.

IN Roman literature, generally, as might be expected, with its more materialistic spirit, the romance of friendship is little dwelt upon; though the grosser side of the passion, in such writers as Catullus and Martial, is much in evidence. Still we find in Virgil a notable instance. His 2nd Eclogue bears the marks of genuine feeling; and, according to some critics, he there under the guise of Shepherd Corydon's love for Alexis celebrates his own attachment to the youthful Alexander:—

"CORYDON, keeper of cattle, once loved the fair lad Alexis; *Virgil Eclogue II*

But he, the delight of his master, permitted no hope to the shepherd.

Corydon, lovesick swain, went into the forest of beeches,

And there to the mountains and woods—the one relief of his passion—

With useless effort outpoured the following artless complainings:—

Alexis, barbarous youth, say, do not my mournful lays move thee?

Showing me no compassion, thou'lt surely compel me to perish.

Even the cattle now seek after places both cool and shady;

Even the lizards green conceal themselves in the thorn-bush.

89

Thestylis, taking sweet herbs, such as garlic and
 thyme, for the reapers
Faint with the scorching noon, doth mash them
 and bray in a mortar.
Alone in the heat of the day am I left with the
 screaming cicalas,
While patient in tracking thy path, I ever pursue
 thee, Belovéd."

Trans. by J. W. Baylis.

There is a translation of this same 2nd Eclogue,
by Abraham Fraunce (1591) which is interesting
not only on account of its felicity of phrase,
but because, as in the case of some other Elizabethan hexameters, the metre is ruled by *quantity, i.e.,*
length of syllables, instead of by *accent.* The following are the first five lines of Fraunce's translation :—

Corydon "SILLY shepherd Corydon lov'd hartyly fayre
and Alexis lad Alexis,
His master's dearling, but saw noe matter of
 hoping;
Only amydst darck groves thickset with broade-
 shadoe beech-trees

Dayly resort did he make, thus alone to the woods,
    to the mountayns,
With broken speeches fond thoughts there vaynly
    revealing."

ATULLUS also (b. B.C. 87) has some
verses of real feeling :—

"QUINTIUS, if 'tis thy wish and *Catullus to*
    will   *Quintius*
  That I should owe my eyes to thee,
Or anything that's dearer still,
  If aught that's dearer there can be;

Then rob me not of that I prize,
  Of the dear form that is to me,
Oh! far far dearer than my eyes,
  Or aught, if dearer aught there be."

        Catullus, trans. Hon. J. Lamb, 1821.

"IF all complying, thou would'st grant   *To*
  Thy lovely eyes to kiss, my fair,   *Juventius*
Long as I pleased; oh! I would plant
  Three hundred thousand kisses there.

Nor could I even then refrain,
  Nor satiate leave that fount of blisses,

Tho' thicker than autumnal grain
    Should be our growing crop of kisses."

(Ibid.)

To "LONG at our leisure yesterday
Licinius   Idling, Licinius, we wrote
Upon my tablets verses gay,
Or took our turns, as fancy smote,
At rhymes and dice and wine.

But when I left, Licinius mine,
Your grace and your facetious mood
Had fired me so, that neither food
Would stay my misery, nor sleep
My roving eyes in quiet keep.
But still consumed, without respite,
I tossed about my couch in vain
And longed for day—if speak I might,
Or be with you again.

But when my limbs with all the strain
Worn out, half dead lay on my bed,
Sweet friend to thee this verse I penned,
That so thou mayest condescend
To understand my pain.

So now, Licinius, beware!
And be not rash, but to my prayer
A gracious hearing tender;

92

Lest on thy head pounce Nemesis:
A goddess sudden and swift she is—
Beware lest thou offend her!"

The following little poem is taken from Martial:

"AS a vineyard breathes, whose boughs with *Martial to*
grapes are bending, *Diadu-*
Or garden where are hived Sicanian bees; *menos*
As upturned clods when summer rain's descending
Or orchards rich with blossom-laden trees;
So, cruel youth, thy kisses breathe—so sweet—
Would'st thou but grant me all their grace,
complete!"

IV.

Friendship in Early
Christian & Mediæval Times

Friendship in Early
Christian & Mediæval Times

THE quotations we have given from Plato and others show the very high ideal of friendship which obtained in the old world, and the respect accorded to it. With the incoming of the Christian centuries, and the growth of Alexandrian and Germanic influences, a change began to take place. Woman rose to greater freedom and dignity and influence than before. The romance of love began to centre round her.[a] The days of chivalry brought a new devotion into the world, and the Church exalted the Virgin Mother to the highest place in heaven. Friendship between men ceased to be regarded in the old light—*i.e.*, as a thing of deep

[a]Benecke, *Woman in Greek Poety* traces a germ of this romance even in Greek days

◺ Sheet Eight

feeling, and an important social institution. It was even, here and there, looked on with disfavour—and lapses from the purity or chastity of its standard were readily suspected and violently reprobated. Certainly it survived in the monastic life for a long period; but though inspiring this to a great extent, its influence was not generally acknowledged. The Family, in the modern and more limited sense of the word (as opposed to the clan), became the recognised unit of social life, and the ideal centre of all good influences (as illustrated in the worship of the Holy Family). At the same time, by this very shrinkage of the Family, as well as by other influences, the solidarity of society became to some extent weakened, and gradually the more communistic forms of the early world gave place to the individualism of the commercial period.

The special sentiment of comrade-love or attachment (being a thing inherent in human nature) remained of course through the Christian centuries, as before, and unaltered—except that being no longer recognised it became a private and personal affair, running often powerfully enough beneath the surface of society, but openly unacknowledged, and so far deprived of some of its dignity and influence. Owing to this fact there is nothing, for this period, to be quoted in the way of general ideal or public opinion on the subject of friendship, and the following sections therefore become limited to the expression of individual sentiments and experiences, in prose and poetry. These we find, during the mediæval period, largely colored by religion; while at the Renaissance and afterwards they are evidently affected by Greek associations.

FOLLOWING are some passages from S. Augustine:—

"IN those years when I first began *Saint* to teach in my native town, I had *Augustine* made a friend, one who through having the same interests was very dear to me, one of my own age, and like me in the first flower of youth. We had grown up together, and went together to school, and used to play together. But he was not yet so great a friend as afterwards, nor even then was our friendship true; for friendship is not true unless

Thou cementest it between those who are united to Thee by that 'love which is shed abroad in our hearts by the Holy Ghost which is given unto us.' Yet our friendship was but too sweet, and fermented by the pursuit of kindred studies. For I had turned him aside from the true faith (of which as a youth he had but an imperfect grasp) to pernicious and superstitious fables, for which my mother grieved over me. And now in mind he erred with me, and my soul could not endure to be separated from him. But lo, Thou didst follow close behind Thy fugitives, Thou—both God of vengeance and fountain of mercies—didst convert us by wonderful ways; behold, Thou didst take him out of this life, when scarcely a year had our close intimacy lasted—sweet to me beyond the sweetness of my whole life. . . . . .

"No ray of light pierced the gloom with which my heart was enveloped by this grief, and wherever I looked I beheld death. My native place was a torment to me, and my father's house strangely joyless; and whatever I had shared with him, without him was now turned into a huge torture. My longing eyes sought him everywhere, and found him not; and I hated the very places, because he was not in them, neither could they say to me 'he is coming,' as they used to do when he was alive and was absent. And I became a great puzzle to myself, and I asked my soul why it was so sad, and why so disquieted within me; and it knew not what to answer. And if I said 'Trust thou in God,' it rightly did not obey; for that dearest one whom it had lost was both truer and better than that phantasm in which it was bidden to trust. Weeping was the only thing which was sweet to me, and it succeeded my friend in the dearest place in my heart." *S. Augustine, Confessions*, bk. 4, ch. iv. *Trans. by Rev. W. H. Hutchings, M.A.*

I WAS miserable, and miserable is every soul *Saint* which is fettered by the love of perishable *Augustine* things; he is torn to pieces when he loses them, and then he perceives how miserable he was in reality while he possessed them. And so was I then, and I wept most bitterly, and in that bitterness I found rest. Thus was I miserable, and that miserable life I held dearer than my friend. For though I would fain have changed it, yet to it I clung even more than to him; and I cannot say whether I would have parted with it for his sake, as it is related, if true, that Orestes and Pylades were willing to do, for they would gladly have died for each other, or together, for they preferred death to separation from each other. But in me a feeling which I cannot explain, and one of a contradictory nature had arisen; for I had at once an unbearable weariness of living, and a fear of dying. For I believe the more I loved him, the more I hated and dreaded death which had taken him from me, and regarded it as a most cruel enemy; and I felt as if it would soon devour all men, now that its power had reached him. ... For I marvelled that other mortals lived, because he whom I had loved, without thought of his ever dying, was dead; and that I still lived—I who was another self—when he was gone, was a greater marvel still. Well said a certain one of his friend, 'Thou half of my soul;' for I felt that his soul and mine were 'one soul in two bodies': and therefore life was to me horrible, because I hated to live as half of a life; and therefore perhaps I feared to die, lest he should wholly die whom I had loved so greatly." *Ibid*, ch. vi.

I T is interesting to see, in these extracts from S. Augustine, and in those which follow from Montalembert, the points of likeness and difference between the Christian ideal of love and that of Plato. Both are highly transcendental, both seem to contemplate an inner union of souls, beyond the reach of space and time; but in Plato the union is in contemplation of the Eternal Beauty, while in the Christian teachers it is in devotion to a personal God.

"IF inanimate nature was to them an abundant *Montalem-* source of pleasure they had a life still more *bert on the* lively and elevated in the life of the heart, in the *Monks* double love which burned in them—the love of their brethren inspired and consecrated by the love of God." *Monks of the West*, introdn., ch. v.

"EVERYTHING invited and encouraged them to choose one or several souls as the intimate companions of their life. . . . And to prove how little the divine love, thus understood and prac- tised, tends to exclude or chill the love of man for man, never was human eloquence more touching or more sincere than in that immortal elegy by which S. Bernard laments a lost brother snatched by death from the cloister :—'Flow, flow my tears, so eager to flow! he who prevented your flowing is here no more! It is not he who is dead, it is I who now live only to die. Why, O why have we loved, and why have we lost each other.'" *Ibid.*

"THE mutual affection which reigned among the monks flowed as a mighty stream through the annals of the cloister. It has left its trace even in the 'formulas,' collected with care by modern erudition. . . . The correspondence of the most illustrious, of Geoffrey de Vendôme, of Pierre le Vénérable, and of S. Bernard, give proofs of it at every page." *Ibid.*

SAINT ANSELM'S letters to brother monks are full of expressions of the same ardent affection. Montalembert gives several examples:—

Saint "SOULS well-beloved of my soul," he wrote to
Anselm two near relatives whom he wished to draw to Bec, "my eyes ardently desire to behold you; my arms expand to embrace you; my lips sigh for your kisses; all the life that remains to me is consumed with waiting for you. I hope in praying, and I pray in hoping—come and taste how gracious the Lord is—you cannot fully know it while you find sweetness in the world."

To his "'FAR from the eyes, far from the heart' say the
Friend vulgar. Believe nothing of it; if it was so, the
Lanfranc farther you were distant from me the cooler my love for you would be; whilst on the contrary, the less I can enjoy your presence, the more the desire of that pleasure burns in the soul of your friend."

"TO Gondulf, Anselm——I put no other or *To* longer salutations at the head of my letter, *Gondulph* because I can say nothing more to him whom I love. All who know Gondulph and Anselm know well what this means, and how much love is understood in these two names." . . . "How could I forget thee? Can a man forget one who is placed like a seal upon his heart? In thy silence I know that thou lovest me; and thou also, when I say nothing, thou knowest that I love thee. Not only have I no doubt of thee, but I answer for thee that thou art sure of me. What can my letter tell thee that thou knowest not already, thou who art my second soul? Go into the secret place of thy heart, look there at thy love for me, and thou shalt see mine for thee." . . . "Thou knewest how much I love thee, but I knew it not. He who has separated us has alone instructed me how dear to me thou wert. No, I knew not before the experience of thy absence how sweet it was to have thee, how bitter to have thee not. Thou hast another friend whom thou hast loved as much or more than me to console thee, but I have no longer thee!—thee! thee! thou understandest? and nothing to replace thee. Those who rejoice in the possession of thee may perhaps be offended by what I say. Ah! let them content themselves with their joy, and permit me to weep for him whom I ever love."

Friendship

THE story of Amis and Amile, a mediæval legend, translated by William Morris (as well as by Walter Pater) from the *Bibliotheca Elzeviriana*, is very quaint and engaging in its old-world extravagance and supernaturalism :—

The Story of Amis and Amile

AMIS and Amile were devoted friends, twins in resemblance and life. On one occasion, having strayed apart, they ceased not to seek each other for two whole years. And when at last they met "they lighted down from their horses, and embraced and kissed each other, and gave thanks to God that they were found. And they swore fealty and friendship and fellowship perpetual, the one to the other, on the sword of Amile, wherein were relics." Thence they went together to the court of "Charles, king of France."

Here soon after, Amis took Amile's place in a tournament, saved his life from a traitor, and won for him the King's daughter to wife. But so it happened that, not long after, he himself was stricken with leprosy and brought to Amile's door. And when Amile and his royal bride knew who it was they were sore grieved, and they brought him in and placed him on a fair bed, and put all that they

106

had at his service. And it came to pass one night "whenas Amis and Amile lay in one chamber without other company, that God sent to Amis Raphael his angel, who said to him: 'Sleepest thou, Amis?' And he, who deemed that Amile had called to him, answered: 'I sleep not, fair sweet fellow.' Then the angel said to him: 'Thou hast answered well, for thou art the fellow of the citizens of heaven, and thou hast followed after Job, and Thoby in patience. Now I am Raphael, an angel of our Lord, and am come to tell thee of a medicine for thine healing, whereas he hath heard thy prayers. Thou shalt tell to Amile thy fellow, that he slay his two children and wash thee in their blood, and thence thou shalt get the healing of thy body.'"

Amis was shocked when he heard these words, and at first refused to tell Amile; but the latter had also heard the angel's voice, and pressed him to tell. Then, when he knew, he too was sorely grieved. But at last he determined in his mind not even to spare his children for the sake of his friend, and going secretly to their chamber he slew them, and bringing some of their blood washed Amis— who immediately was healed. He then arrayed Amis in his best clothes and, after going to the church to give thanks, they met Amile's wife who

Friendship

(not knowing all) rejoiced greatly too. But Amile, going apart again to the children's chamber to weep over them, found them at play in bed, with only a thread of crimson round their throats to mark what had been done!

The two knights fell afterwards and were killed in the same battle; "for even as God had joined them together by good accord in their life-days, so in their death they were not sundered." And a miracle was added, for even when they were buried apart from each other the two coffins leapt together in the night and were found side by side in the morning.

Of this story Mr. Jacobs, in his introduction to William Morris' translation, says: "Amis and Amil were the David and Jonathan, the Orestes and Pylades, of the mediæval world." There were some thirty other versions of the legend "in almost all the tongues of Western and Northern Europe"— their "peerless friendship" having given them a place among the mediæval saints. (See *Old French Romances* trans. by William Morris, London, 1896.)

Eastern Countries

IT may not be out of place here, and before passing on to the times of the Renaissance and Modern Europe, to give one or two extracts relating to Eastern countries. The honour paid to friendship in Persia, Arabia, Syria and other Oriental lands has always been great, and the tradition of this attachment there should be especially interesting to us, as having arisen independently of classic or Christian ideals. The poets of Persia, Saadi and Jelal-ud-din Rumi (13th cent.), Hafiz (14th cent.), Jami (15th cent.), and others, have drawn much of their inspiration from this source; but unfortunately for those who cannot read the originals, their work has been scantily translated, and the translations themselves are not always very reliable. The extraordinary way in which, following the method of the Sufis, and of Plato, they identify the mortal and the divine love, and see in their beloved an image or revelation of God himself, makes their poems difficult of comprehension to the Western mind. Apostrophes to Love, Wine, and Beauty often, with them, bear a frankly twofold sense, material and spiritual. To these poets of the mid-region of the earth, the bitter antagonism between matter and spirit, which like an evil dream has *Jalalu-* haunted so long both the extreme Western and the *ddin* extreme Eastern mind, scarcely exists; and even the *Rumi* body "which is a portion of the dust-pit" has become perfect and divine.

"EVERY form you see has its archetype in the placeless world. . . .

From the moment you came into the world of being

A ladder was placed before you that you might escape (ascend).

First you were mineral, later you turned to plant,

Then you became an animal: how should this be a secret to you?

Afterwards you were made man, with knowledge, reason, faith;

Behold the body, which is a portion of the dust-pit, how perfect it has grown!

When you have travelled on from man, you will doubtless become an angel;

110

pined away to absolute illness, and was near following the fate of him whom he deplored." *Ibid*, p.16c.

"FROM all this, added to many other examples *Explana-* of a similar kind, related as happening be- *tion* tween persons who had often been pointed out to me in Arabia and Persia, I could no longer doubt the existence in the East of an affection for male youths, of as pure and honorable a kind as that which is felt in Europe for those of the other sex ... and it would be as unjust to suppose that this necessarily implied impurity of desire as to contend that no one could admire a lovely countenance and a beautiful form in the other sex, and still be inspired with sentiments of the most pure and honorable nature towards the object of his admiration." *Ibid*, p. 163.

"ONE powerful reason why this passion may exist in the East, while it is quite unknown in the West, is probably the seclusion of women in the former, and the freedom of access to them in the latter. . . . Had they [the Asiatics] the unrestrained intercourse which we enjoy with such superior beings as the virtuous and accomplished females of our own country they would find nothing in nature so deserving of their love as these." *Ibid*, p. 165.

Friendship

There is no room for the raw at my well-cooked
 feast.
Naught but fire of separation and absence
Can cook the raw one and free him from hypocrisy!
Since thy *self* has not yet left thee,
Thou must be burned in fiery flames.'
The poor man went away, and for one whole year
Journeyed burning with grief for his friend's
 absence.
His heart burned till it was cooked; then he went
 again
And drew near to the house of his friend.
He knocked at the door in fear and trepidation
Lest some careless word should fall from his lips.
His friend shouted, 'Who is that at the door?'
He answered, ''Tis thou who art at the door, O
 beloved!'
The friend said, 'Since 'tis I, let me come in,
There is not room for two I's in one house.'"

*From the Masnavi of Jalalu-ddin
Rumi, trans. by E. H. Whinfield.*

SOME short quotations here following
are taken from *Flowers culled from
Persian Gardens* (Manchester, 1872):

"EVERYONE, whether he be
abstemious or self-indulgent

is searching after the Friend. Every place may be *Hafiz and* the abode of love, whether it be a mosque or a sy- *Saadis* nagogue. . . . On thy last day, though the cup be in thy hand, thou may'st be borne away to Paradise even from the corner of the tavern." *Hafiz.*

"I HAVE heard a sweet word which was spoken by the old man of Canaan (Jacob)—'No tongue can express what means the separation of friends.'" *Hafiz.*

"NEITHER of my own free will cast I myself into the fire; for the chain of affection was laid upon my neck. I was still at a distance when the fire began to glow, nor is this the moment that it was lighted up within me. Who shall impute it to me as a fault, that I am enchanted by my friend, that I am content in casting myself at his feet?" *Saadi.*

Hahn in his *Albanesische Studien*, already quoted (p. 20), gives some of the verses of Neçin or Nesim Bey, a Turco-Albanian poet, of which the following is an example:—

"WHATE'ER, my friend, or false or true,
     The world may tell thee, give no ear,
For to separate us, dear,
The world will say that one is two.

113   ◢ SHEET NINE

Friendship

Who should seek to separate us
    May he never cease to weep.
The rain at times may cease; but he
    In Summer's warmth or Winter's sleep
    May he never cease to weep."

BESIDES literature there is no doubt a vast amount of material embedded in the customs and traditions of these countries and awaiting adequate recognition and interpretation. The following quotations may afford some glimpses of interest.

Suleyman the Magnificent.—The story of Suleyman's attachment to his Vezir Ibrahim is told as follows by Stanley Lane-Poole:—

Suleyman and Ibrahim "SULEYMAN, great as he was, shared his greatness with a second mind, to which his reign owed much of its brilliance. The Grand Vezir Ibrahim was the counterpart of the Grand Monarch Suleyman. He was the son of a sailor at Parga, and had been captured by corsairs, by whom he was sold to be the slave of a widow at Magnesia. Here he passed into the hands of the young prince Suleyman, then Governor of Magnesia, and soon his extraordinary talents and address brought him promotion.... From being Grand Falconer on the

114

accession of Suleyman, he rose to be first minister and almost co-Sultan in 1523.

"He was the object of the Sultan's tender regard: an emperor knows better than most men how solitary is life without friendship and love, and Suleyman loved this man more than a brother. Ibrahim was not only a friend, he was an entertaining and instructive companion. He read Persian, Greek and Italian; he knew how to open unknown worlds to the Sultan's mind, and Suleyman drank in his Vezir's wisdom with assiduity. They lived together: their meals were shared in common; even their beds were in the same room. The Sultan gave his sister in marriage to the sailor's son, and Ibrahim was at the summit of power." *Turkey, Story of Nations series*, p. 174.

. S. BUCKINGHAM, in his *Travels in Assyria, Media and Persia*, speaking of his guide whom he had engaged at Bagdad, and who was supposed to have left his heart behind him in that city, says :—

"AMIDST all this I was at a loss to conceive how the Dervish could find much enjoyment [in the expedition] while laboring under the strong passion which I supposed he must then be feeling for the object of his affections at Bagdad, whom he had quitted with so much reluctance. What was my surprise however on seeking an explanation of this seeming inconsistency, to find it was the son, and not the daughter, of his friend Elias who held so powerful a hold on his heart. I shrank back from the confession as a man would recoil from a serpent on which he had unexpectedly trodden ... but in answer to enquiries naturally suggested by the subject he declared he would rather suffer death than do the slightest harm to so pure, so innocent, so heavenly a creature as this. ...

"I took the greatest pains to ascertain by a severe and minute investigation, how far it might be possible to doubt of the purity of the passion by which this Affgan Dervish was possessed, and whether it deserved to be classed with that described as prevailing among the ancient Greeks; and the result fully satisfied me that both were the same. Ismael was however surprised beyond measure when I assured him that such a feeling was not known at all among the peoples of Europe." *Travels, &c.,* 2nd edition, vol. 1, p. 159.

"THE Dervish added a striking instance of the force of these attachments, and the sympathy which was felt in the sorrows to which they led, by the following fact from his own history. The place

of his residence, and of his usual labour, was near *Another*
the bridge of the Tigris, at the gate of the Mosque *Story*
of the Vizier. While he sat here, about five or six
years since, surrounded by several of his friends
who came often to enjoy his conversation and
beguile the tedium of his work, he observed, passing among the crowd, a young and beautiful
Turkish boy, whose eyes met his, as if by destiny,
and they remained fixedly gazing on each other for
some time. The boy, after 'blushing like the first
hue of a summer morning,' passed on, frequently
turning back to look on the person who had regarded him so ardently. The Dervish felt his heart
'revolve within him,' for such was his expression,
and a cold sweat came across his brow. He hung
his head upon his graving-tool in dejection, and ex-
cused himself to those about him by saying he felt
suddenly ill. Shortly afterwards the boy returned,
and after walking to and fro several times, drawing
nearer and nearer, as if under the influence of some
attracting charm, he came up to his observer and
said, 'Is it really true, then, that you love me?'
'This,' said Ismael, 'was a dagger in my heart;
I could make no reply.' The friends who were near
him, and now saw all explained, asked him if there
had been any previous acquaintance existing between them. He assured them that they had never

seen each other before. 'Then,' they replied, 'such an event must be from God.'

"The boy continued to remain for a while with this party, told with great frankness the name and rank of his parents, as well as the place of his residence, and promised to repeat his visit on the following day. He did this regularly for several months in succession, sitting for hours by the Dervish, and either singing to him or asking him interesting questions, to beguile his labours, until as Ismael expressed himself, 'though they were still two bodies they became one soul.' The youth at length fell sick, and was confined to his bed, during which time his lover, Ismael, discontinued entirely his usual occupations and abandoned himself completely to the care of his beloved. He watched the changes of his disease with more than the anxiety of a parent, and never quitted his bedside, night or day. Death at length separated them; but even when the stroke came the Dervish could not be prevailed on to quit the corpse. He constantly visited the grave that contained the remains of all he held dear on earth, and planting myrtles and flowers there after the manner of the East, bedewed them daily with his tears. His friends sympathised powerfully in his distress, which he said 'continued to feed his grief' until he pined away to absolute illness, and was near following the fate of him whom he deplored." *Ibid*, p.160.

"FROM all this, added to many other examples *Explana* of a similar kind, related as happening be- *tion* tween persons who had often been pointed out to me in Arabia and Persia, I could no longer doubt the existence in the East of an affection for male youths, of as pure and honorable a kind as that which is felt in Europe for those of the other sex . . . and it would be as unjust to suppose that this necessarily implied impurity of desire as to contend that no one could admire a lovely countenance and a beautiful form in the other sex, and still be inspired with sentiments of the most pure and honorable nature towards the object of his admiration." *Ibid*, p. 163.

"ONE powerful reason why this passion may exist in the East, while it is quite unknown in the West, is probably the seclusion of women in the former, and the freedom of access to them in the latter. . . . Had they [the Asiatics] the unrestrained intercourse which we enjoy with such superior beings as the virtuous and accomplished females of our own country they would find nothing in nature so deserving of their love as these." *Ibid*, p. 165.

V.

The Renaissance
and Modern Times

The Renaissance
and Modern Times

ITH the Renaissance, and the impetus it gave at that time to the study of Greek and Roman models, the exclusive domination of Christianity and the Church was broken. A literature of friendship along classic lines began to spring up. Montaigne (b. 1533) was saturated with classic learning. His essays were doubtless largely formed upon the model of Plutarch. His friendship with Stephen de la Boëtie was evidently of a romantic and absorbing character. It is referred to in the following passage by William Hazlitt; and the description of it occupies a large part of Montaigne's Essay on Friendship.

Friendship

Montaigne and Stephen de la Boëtie

^a"De la Servitude Volontaire"

"THE most important event of his counsellor's life at Bordeaux was the friendship which he there formed with Stephen de la Boëtie, an affection which makes a streak of light in modern biography almost as beautiful as that left us by Lord Brook and Sir Philip Sydney. Our essayist and his friend esteemed, before they saw, each other. La Boëtie had written a little work^a in which Montaigne recognised sentiments congenial with his own, and which indeed bespeak a soul formed in the mould of classic times. Of Montaigne, la Boëtie had also heard accounts, which made him eager to behold him, and at length they met at a large entertainment given by one of the magistrates of Bordeaux. They saw and loved, and were thenceforward all in all to each other. The picture that Montaigne in his essays draws of this friendship is in the highest degree beautiful and touching; nor does la Boëtie's idea of what is due to this sacred bond betwixt soul and soul fall far short of the grand perception which filled the exalted mind of his friend. . . . Montaigne married at the age of 33, but, as he informs us, not of his own wish or choice. 'Might I have had my wish,' says he, 'I would not have married Wisdom herself if she would have had me.'" *Life of Montaigne, by Wm. Hazlitt.*

The following is from Montaigne's Essay, bk. 1, ch. xxvii:—

"AS to marriage, besides that it is a covenant, *Montaigne* the *making* of which is only free, but the con- *on* tinuance in it forced and compelled, having an- *Friendship* other dependence than that of our own free will, and a bargain moreover commonly contracted to other ends, there happen a thousand intricacies in it to unravel, enough to break the thread, and to divert the current, of a lively affection: whereas friendship has no manner of business or traffic with anything but itself. . . . For the rest, what we commonly call friends and friendships are nothing but an acquaintance and connection, contracted either by accident or upon some design, by means of which there happens some little intercourse betwixt our souls: but, in the friendship I speak of, they mingle and melt into one piece, with so universal a mixture that there is left no more sign of the seam by which they were first conjoined. If any one should importune me to give a reason why I loved him [Stephen de la Boëtie] I feel it could no otherwise be expressed than by making answer, 'Because it was he; because it was I.' There is, beyond what I am able to say, I know not what inexplicable and inevitable power that brought on this union. We sought one another long before we met, and from the characters we heard of one another, which wrought more upon our affections than in reason mere reports should do, and, as I think, by some secret appointment of heaven; we embraced each other in our names; and at our first meeting, which was accidentally at a great city entertainment, we found ourselves so mutually pleased with one another—we became at once mutually so endeared—that thenceforward nothing was so near to us as one another. . . .

"Common friendships will admit of division, one may love the beauty of this, the good humour of that person, the liberality of a third, the paternal affection of a fourth, the fraternal love of a fifth, and so on. But this friendship that possesses the whole soul, and there rules and sways with an absolute sovereignty, can admit of no rival. . . . In good earnest, if I compare all the rest of my life with the four years I had the happiness to enjoy the sweet society of this excellent man, 'tis nothing but smoke, but an obscure and tedious night. From the day that I lost him I have only led a sorrowful and languishing life; and the very pleasures that present themselves to me, instead of administering anything of consolation, double my affliction for his loss. We were halves throughout, and to that degree that, methinks, by outliving him I defraud him of his part."

PHILIP SIDNEY, born 1554, was remarkable for his strong personal attachments. Chief among his allies were his school-mate and distant relative, Fulke Greville (born in the same year as himself), and his college friend Edward Dyer (also about his own age). He wrote youthful verses to both of them. The following, according to the fashion of the age, are in the form of an invocation to the pastoral god Pan:—

> "ONLY for my two loves' sake,
> In whose love I pleasure take;
> Only two do me delight
> With their ever-pleasing sight;
> Of all men to thee retaining
> Grant me with these two remaining."

*Sidney
Greville
and Dyer*

An interesting friendship existed also between Sidney and the well-known French Protestant, Hubert Languet—many years his senior—whose conversation and correspondence helped much in the formation of Sidney's character. These two had shared together the perils of the massacre of S. Bartholomew, and had both escaped from France across the Rhine to Germany, where they lived in close intimacy at Frankfort for a length of time; and after this a warm friendship and steady correspondence— varied by occasional meetings—continued between the two until Languet's death. Languet had been Professor of Civil Law at Padua, and from 1550 forwards was recognised as one of the leading political agents of the Protestant Powers.

Philip Sidney and Hubert Languet "THE elder man immediately discerned in Sidney a youth of no common quality, and the attachment he conceived for him savoured of romance. We possess a long series of Latin letters from Languet to his friend, which breathe the tenderest spirit of affection, mingled with wise counsel and ever watchful thought for the young man's higher interests. . . . There must have been something inexplicably attractive in his [Sidney's] person and his genius at this time; for the tone of Languet's correspondence can only be matched by that of Shakespeare in the sonnets written for his unknown friend." *Sir Philip Sidney, English Men of Letters Series*, pp. 27, 28.

Of this relation Fox Bourne says :—

"NO love-oppressed youth can write with more earnest passion and more fond solicitude, or can be troubled with more frequent fears and more causeless jealousies, than Languet, at this time 55 years old, shows in his letters to Sidney, now 19."

IT may be appropriate here to introduce two or three sonnets from Michel Angelo (b. 1475). Michel Angelo, one of the greatest, perhaps the greatest, artist of the Italian Renaissance, was deeply imbued with the Greek spirit. His conception of Love was close along the line of Plato's. For him the body was the symbol, the expression, the dwelling place of some divine beauty. The body may be loved, but it should only be loved *as* a symbol, not for itself. Diotima in the *Symposium* had said that in our mortal loves we first come to recognise (dimly) the divine form of beauty which is Eternal. Maximus Tyrius (Dissert. xxvi. 8) commenting on this, confirms it, saying that nowhere else but in the human form, "the loveliest and most intelligent of bodily creatures," does the light of divine beauty shine so clear. Michel Angelo carried on the conception, gave it noble expression, and held to it firmly in the midst of a society which was certainly willing enough to love the body (or try to love it) merely for its own sake. And Giordano Bruno (b. 1550) at a later date wrote as follows:—

Giordano Bruno "ALL the loves—if they be heroic and not purely animal, or what is called natural, and slaves to generation as instruments in some way of nature—have for object the divinity, and tend towards divine beauty, which first is communicated to, and shines in, souls, and from them or rather through them is communicated to bodies; whence it is that well-ordered affection loves the body or corporeal beauty, insomuch as it is an indication of beauty of spirit." *Gli Eroici Furori* (dial. iii. 13), *trans. L. Williams.*

THE labours of Von Scheffler and others have now pretty conclusively established that the love-poems of Michel Angelo were for the most

part written to male friends—though this fact was disguised by the pious frauds of his nephew, who edited them in the first instance. Following are three of his sonnets, translated by J. A. Symonds. It will be seen that the last line of the first contains a play on the name of his friend :—

To Tommaso de' Cavalieri:
A CHE PIU DEBB'IO.

"WHY should I seek to ease intense desire   *Michel*
    With still more tears and windy words of *Angelo's*
    grief,   *Sonnets*
  When heaven, or late or soon, sends no relief
  To souls whom love hath robed around with
    fire.
Why need my aching heart to death aspire,
  When all must die? Nay death beyond belief
  Unto these eyes would be both sweet and brief,
  Since in my sum of woes all joys expire!

Therefore because I cannot shun the blow
  I rather seek, say who must rule my breast,
  Gliding between her gladness and her woe?
If only chains and bands can make me blest,
  No marvel if alone and bare I go
  An armèd Knight's captive and slave confessed."

Friendship

"NO mortal thing enthralled these longing eyes
    When perfect peace in thy fair face I found;
But far within, where all is holy ground,
My soul felt Love, her comrade of the skies:
For she was born with God in Paradise;
    Nor all the shows of beauty shed around
    This fair false world her wings to earth have
        bound;
Unto the Love of Loves aloft she flies.

Nay, things that suffer death quench not the fire
    Of deathless spirits; nor eternity
Serves sordid Time, that withers all things rare.
Not love but lawless impulse is desire:
    That slays the soul; our love makes still more
        fair
    Our friends on earth, fairer in death on high."

"FROM thy fair face I learn, O my loved lord,
    That which no mortal tongue can rightly say;
The soul imprisoned in her house of clay,
Holpen by thee to God hath often soared:
And tho' the vulgar, vain, malignant horde
    Attribute what their grosser wills obey,
    Yet shall this fervent homage that I pay,
This love, this faith, pure joys for us afford.

Lo, all the lovely things we find on earth,
   Resemble for the soul that rightly sees,
   That source of bliss divine which gave us birth :
Nor have we first fruits or remembrances
   Of heaven elsewhere. Thus, loving loyally,
   I rise to God and make death sweet by thee."

RICHARD BARNFIELD, one of the Elizabethan singers (b. 1574) wrote a long poem, dedicated to "The Ladie Penelope Rich" and entitled "The Affectionate Shepheard," which he describes as "an imitation of Virgil in the 2nd Eclogue, of Alexis." I quote the first two stanzas :—

I.

"SCARCE had the morning starre hid from the   *Richard*
   light   *Barnfield*
Heaven's crimson Canopie with stars bespangled,
But I began to rue th' unhappy sight
Of that fair boy that had my heart intangled;
   Cursing the Time, the Place, the sense, the sin;
   I came, I saw, I view'd, I slippèd in.

133

Friendship

II.

If it be sin to love a sweet-fac'd Boy,
(Whose amber locks trust up in golden tramels
Dangle adown his lovely cheekes with joye
When pearle and flowers his faire haire enamels)
   If it be sin to love a lovely Lad,
    Oh then sinne I, for whom my soule is sad."

These stanzas, and the following three sonnets
(also by Barnfield) from a series addressed to a
youth, give a fair sample of a considerable class of
Elizabethan verses, in which classic conceits were
mingled with a certain amount of real feeling:—

Sonnet IV.

Barnfield's "TWO stars there are in one fair firmament
Sonnets   (Of some intitled Ganymede's sweet face)
   Which other stars in brightness do disgrace,
As much as Po in cleanness passeth Trent.
Nor are they common-natur'd stars; for why,
   These stars when other shine vaile their pure
    light,
   And when all other vanish out of sight
They add a glory to the world's great eie:

By these two stars my life is only led,
  In them I place my joy, in them my pleasure,
  Love's piercing darts and Nature's precious
    treasure,
With their sweet food my fainting soul is fed:
  Then when my sunne is absent from my sight
  How can it chuse (with me) but be darke night?"

Sonnet XVIII.

"NOT Megabetes, nor Cleonymus
  (Of whom great Plutarch makes such
    mention,
  Praysing their faire with rare invention),
As Ganymede were halfe so beauteous.
They onely pleased the eies of two great kings,
  But all the world at my love stands amazed,
  Nor one that on his angel's face hath gazed,
But (ravisht with delight) him presents bring:

Some weaning lambs, and some a suckling kyd,
  Some nuts, and fil-beards, others peares and
    plums;
  Another with a milk-white heyfar comes;
As lately Ægon's man (Damœtas) did;
  But neither he nor all the Nymphs beside,
  Can win my Ganymede with them t' abide."

135

Friendship

Sonnet XIX.

"AH no; nor I my selfe: tho' my pure love
  (Sweete Ganymede) to thee hath still been
    pure,
  And ev'n till my last gaspe shall aie endure,
Could ever thy obdurate beuty move:
Then cease, oh goddesse sonne (for sure thou art
  A Goddesse sonne that can resist desire),
  Cease thy hard heart, and entertain love's fire
Within thy sacred breast: by Nature's art.

And as I love thee more than any Creature
  (Love thee, because thy beautie is divine,
  Love thee, because my selfe, my soule, is thine:
Wholie devoted to thy lovely feature),
  Even so of all the vowels, I and U
  Are dearest unto me, as doth ensue."

FRANCIS BACON'S essay *Of friendship* is known to everybody. Notwithstanding the somewhat cold and pragmatic style and genius of the author, the subject seems to inspire him with a certain enthusiasm; and some good things are said

'BUT we may go farther and affirm most truly *Francis* that it is a mere and miserable solitude to want *Bacon on* true friends, without which the world is but a *Friendship* wilderness; and even in this scene also of solitude, whosoever in the frame of his nature and affections is unfit for friendship, he taketh it of the beast, and not from humanity. A principal fruit of friendship is the ease and discharge of the fulness of the heart, which passions of all kinds do cause and induce. We know diseases of stoppings and suffocations are the most dangerous in the body; and it is not much otherwise in the mind: you may take sarza to open the liver, steel to open the spleen, flower of sulphur for the lungs, castoreum for the brain; but no receipt openeth the heart but a true friend, to whom you may impart griefs, joys, fears, hopes, suspicions, counsels, and whatsoever lieth upon the heart to oppress it, in a kind of civil shrift or confession. . . .

"Certainly if a man would give it a hard phrase, those that want friends to open themselves unto, are cannibals of their own hearts; but one thing is most admirable (wherewith I will conclude this first fruit of friendship) which is, that this communicating of a man's self to his friend worketh two contrary effects, for it redoubleth joys, and cutteth griefs in halfs; for there is no man that imparteth his joys to his friend, but he joyeth the more, and no man that imparteth his griefs to his friend, but he grieveth the less." Essay 27, *Of friendship*.

SHAKESPEARE'S sonnets have been much discussed, and surprise and even doubt have been expressed as to their having been addressed (the first 126 of them) to a man friend; but no one who reads them with open mind can well doubt this conclusion; nor be surprised at it, who knows anything of Elizabethan life and literature. "Were it not for the fact," says F. T. Furnivall, "that many critics really deserving the name of Shakespeare students, and not Shakespeare fools, have held the Sonnets to be merely dramatic, I could not have conceived that poems so intensely and evidently autobiographic and self-revealing, poems so one with the spirit and inner meaning of Shakespeare's growth and life, could ever have been conceived to be other than what they are—the records of his own loves and fears."

Sonnet XVIII.

"SHALL I compare thee to a summer's day?
Thou art more lovely and more temperate:
Rough winds do shake the darling buds of May,
And summer's lease hath all too short a date.
Some time too hot the eye of heaven shines,
And often is his gold complexion dimmed;
And every fair from fair sometime declines,
By chance, or nature's changing course, un-
    trimmed;
But thy eternal summer shall not fade,
Nor lose possession of that fair thou owest;
Nor shall death brag thou wander'st in his shade,
When in eternal lines to time thou growest.
    So long as men can breathe, or eyes can see,
    So long lives this, and this gives life to thee."

*Shakes-
peare's
Sonnets*

Sonnet XX.

"A WOMAN'S face, with Nature's own hand
    painted,
Hast thou, the master-mistress of my passion;
A woman's gentle heart, but not acquainted
With shifting change, as is false women's fashion;
An eye more bright than theirs, less false in rolling,
Gilding the object whereupon it gazeth;
A man in hue, all hues in his controlling,
Which steals men's eyes, and women's souls ama-
    zeth;   139

And for a woman wert thou first created;
Till Nature, as she wrought thee, fell a-doting,
And by addition me of thee defeated,
By adding one thing to my purpose nothing.
    But since she pricked thee out for women's
        pleasure,
    Mine be thy love, and thy love's use their
        treasure."

Sonnet CIV.

'TO me, fair friend, you never can be old,
    For as you were when first your eye I ey'd,
Such seems your beauty still. Three winters cold
Have from the forest shook three summers' pride;
Three beauteous springs to yellow autumn turned
In process of the seasons I have seen;
Three April perfumes in three hot Junes burned,
Since first I saw you fresh, which yet are green.

Ah! yet doth beauty, like a dial hand,
Steal from his figure, and no pace perceived;
So your sweet hue, which methinks still doth
        stand,
Hath motion, and mine eye may be deceived;
    For fear of which, hear this, thou age unbred,
    Ere you were born was beauty's summer dead."

Sonnet CVIII.

"WHAT'S in the brain that ink may character,
　　Which hath not figur'd to thee my true
　　　　spirit?
What's new to speak, what new to register,
That may express my love, or thy dear merit?
Nothing, sweet boy; but yet, like prayers divine,
I must each day say o'er the very same,
Counting no old thing old, thou mine, I thine,
Even as when first I hallow'd thy fair name.

So that eternal love, in love's fresh case,
Weighs not the dust and injury of age;
Nor gives to necessary wrinkles place,
But makes antiquity for aye his page;
　　Finding the first conceit of love there bred,
　　Where time and outward form would show it
　　　　dead."

THAT Shakespeare, when the drama needed it, could fully and warmly enter into the devotion which one man may feel for another, as well as into the tragedy which such devotion may entail, is shown in his *Merchant of Venice* by the figure of

Antonio, over whom from the first line of the play ("In sooth I know not why I am so sad") there hangs a shadow of destiny. The following lines are from Act iv. sc. 1 :—

Merchant of Venice

Antonio: "COMMEND me to your honorable wife;
Tell her the process of Antonio's end;
Say how I loved you, speak me fair in death;
And when the tale is told, bid her be judge,
Whether Bassanio had not once a love.
Repent not you that you shall lose your friend,
And he repents not that he pays your debt;
For, if the Jew do cut but deep enough,
I'll pay it instantly with all my heart.

Bassanio: Antonio, I am married to a wife,
Who is as dear to me as life itself;
But life itself, my wife, and all the world,
Are not with me esteem'd above thy life:
I would lose all, ay, sacrifice them all,
Here to this devil, to deliver you."

We may also, in this connection, quote his *Henry the Fifth* (act iv. scene 6) for the deaths of the Duke

of York and the Earl of Suffolk at the battle of
Agincourt. Exeter, addressing Henry, says :—

"SUFFOLK first died; and York, all haggled   *Henry the*
over,   *Fifth*
Comes to him, where in gore he lay insteep'd,
And takes him by the beard, kisses the gashes,
That bloodily did yawn upon his face;
He cries aloud,—'Tarry, dear cousin Suffolk!
My soul shall thine keep company to heaven:
Tarry, sweet soul, for mine; then fly abreast,
As in this glorious and well-foughten field
We kept together in our chivalry!'
Upon these words I came and cheered him up:
He smiled me in the face, raught me his hand,
And, with a feeble gripe, says, 'Dear my Lord,
Commend my service to my sovereign.'
So did he turn, and over Suffolk's neck
He threw his wounded arm, and kissed his lips;
And so, espoused to death, with blood he seal'd
A testament of noble-ending love."

Shakespeare, with his generous many-sided nature
was, as the Sonnets seem to show, and as we should
expect, capable of friendship, passionate friendship,
towards both men and women. Perhaps this marks

143

the highest reach of temperament. That there are cases in which devotion to a man-friend altogether replaces the love of the opposite sex is curiously shown by the following extract from Sir Thomas Browne:—

Sir "I NEVER yet cast a true affection on a woman;
Thomas but I have loved my friend as I do virtue, my
Browne soul, my God. . . . I love my friend before myself, and yet methinks I do not love him enough: some few months hence my multiplied affection will make me believe I have not loved him at all. When I am from him, I am dead till I be with him; when I am with him, I am not satisfied, but would be still nearer him. . . . This noble affection falls not on vulgar and common constitutions, but on such as are marked for virtue: he that can love his friend with this noble ardour, will in a competent degree affect all." *Sir Thomas Browne, Religio Medici*, 1642.

WILLIAM PENN (b. 1644) the foun-
der of Pennsylvania, and of Philadelphia, "The city of brotherly love"
was a great believer in friendship.
He says in his *Fruits of Solitude*:—

"A TRUE friend unbosoms freely, advises *William* justly, assists readily, adventures boldly, *Penn* takes all patiently, defends courageously, and continues a friend unchangeably. . . . In short, choose a friend as thou dost a wife, till death separate you. . . . Death cannot kill what never dies. Nor can spirits ever be divided that love and live in the same Divine Principle; the Root and Record of their friendship. . . . This is the comfort of friends, that though they may be said to die, yet their friendship and society are, in the best sense, ever present, because immortal."

IT may be worth while here to insert two passages from Macaulay's History of England. The first deals with the remarkable intimacy between the Young Prince William of Orange and "a gentleman of his household" named Bentinck. William's escape from a malignant attack of small-pox

"was attributed partly to his own singular equanimity, and partly to the intrepid and indefatigable friendship of Bentinck. From the hands of Bentinck alone William took food and medicine—by Bentinck alone William was lifted from his bed and laid down in it. 'Whether Bentinck slept or

William of Orange

145

not while I was ill,' said William to Temple with
great tenderness, 'I know not. But this I know,
that through sixteen days and nights, I never once
called for anything but that Bentinck was instantly
at my side.' Before the faithful servant had entirely performed his task, he had himself caught
the contagion." (But he recovered.) *History of
England*, ch. vii.

The second passage describes the devotion of the
Princess Anne (daughter of James II. and afterwards Queen Anne) to Lady Churchill—a devotion
which had considerable influence on the political
situation.

*Princess
Anne and
Lady
Churchill*
"IT is a common observation that differences of
taste, understanding, and disposition are no
impediments to friendship, and that the closest in-
timacies often exist between minds, each of which
supplies what is wanting in the other. Lady
Churchill was loved and even worshipped by
Anne. The princess could not live apart from the
object of her romantic fondness. She married, and
was a faithful and even an affectionate wife; but
Prince George, a dull man, whose chief pleasures
were derived from his dinner and his bottle, acquired over her no influence comparable to that

exercised by her female friend, and soon gave himself up with stupid patience to the dominion of that vehement and commanding spirit by which his wife was governed." *History of England*, ch. vii.

THAT the tradition of Greek thought was not quite obliterated in England by the Puritan movement is shown by the writings of Archbishop Potter, who speaks with approval of friendship as followed among the Greeks, "not only in private, but by the *Archbishop* public allowance and encouragement of their laws, *Potter* for they thought there could be no means more effectual to excite their youth to noble undertakings, nor any greater security to their commonwealths, than this generous passion." He then quotes Athenæus, saying that "free commonwealths and all those states that consulted the advancement of their own honour, seem to have been unanimous in establishing laws to encourage and reward it." *John Potter, Antiquities of Greece*, 1698.

The 18th century however in England, with its leaning towards formalism, was perhaps not

147

favorable to the understanding of the Greek spirit. At any rate there is not much to show in that direction. In Germany the classical tradition in art was revived by Raphael Mengs, while Winckelmann, the art critic, showed himself one of the best interpreters of the Hellenic world that has ever lived. His letters too, to his personal friends, breathe a spirit of the tenderest and most passionate devotion: "Friendship," he says, "without love is mere acquaintanceship." Winckelmann met, in 1762, in Rome, a young nobleman, Reinhold von Berg, to whom he became deeply attached:—

Winckel-mann's Letters

"ALMOST at first sight there sprang up, on Winckelmann's side, an attachment as romantic, emotional and passionate as love. In a letter to his friend he said, 'From the first moment an indescribable attraction towards you, excited by something more than form and feature, caused me to catch an echo of that harmony which passes human understanding and which is the music of the everlasting concord of things. . . . I was aware of the deep consent of our spirits, the instant I saw you.' And in a later letter: 'No name by which I might call you would be sweet enough or suffi-

148

cient for my love; all that I could say would be far
too feeble to give utterance to my heart and soul.
Truly friendship came from heaven and was not
created by mere human impulses. . . . My one
friend, I love you more than any living thing, and
time nor chance nor age can ever lessen this love."
Ludwig Frey, Der Eros und die Kunst, Leipzig,
1898, p. 211.

GOETHE, that universal genius, has
some excellent thoughts on this subject; speaking of Winckelmann he
says:—

"THE affinities of human beings in Antiquity *Goethe on*
give evidence of an important distinction be- *Winckel-*
tween ancient and modern times. The relation to *mann*
women, which among us has become so tender and
full of meaning, hardly aspired in those days beyond the limits of vulgar necessity. The relation
of parents to their children seems in some respects
to have been tenderer. More to them than all other
feelings was the friendship between persons of the
male sex (though female friends too, like Chloris
and Thyia, were inseparable, even in Hades). In
these cases of union between two youths, the
passionate fulfilment of loving duties, the joys of

149

inseparableness, the devotion of one for the other, the unavoided companionship in death, fill us with astonishment; indeed one feels oneself ashamed when poets, historians, philosophers and orators overwhelm us with legends, anecdotes, sentiments and ideas, containing such meaning and feeling. Winckelmann felt himself *born* for a friendship of this kind—not only as capable of it, but in the highest degree in need of it; he became conscious of his true self only under the form of friendship."
Goethe on Winckelmann.

Some of Goethe's poems further illustrate this subject. In the Saki Nameh of his West-Oestlichen Divan he has followed the style of a certain class of Persian love-songs. The following poem is from a Cupbearer to his Master:—

Poem by Goethe

"IN the market-place appearing
   None thy Poet-fame dispute;
I too gladly hear thy singing,
   I too hearken when thou'rt mute.

Yet I love thee, when thou printest
   Kisses not to be forgot,
Best of all, for words may perish,
   But a kiss lives on in thought.

Rhymes on rhymes fair meaning carry,
    Thoughts to think bring deeper joy;
Sing to other folk, but tarry
    Silent with thy serving-boy."

COUNT AUGUST VON PLATEN (born at Ansbach in Bavaria, 1796) was in respect of style one of the most finished and perfect of German poets. His nature (which was refined and self-controlled) led him from the first to form the most romantic attachments with men. He freely and openly expressed his feelings in his verses; of which a great number are practically love-poems addressed to his friends. They include a series of twenty-six sonnets to one of his friends, Karl Theodor German. Of these Raffalovich says (*Uranisme*, Lyons, 1896, p. 351):—

"THESE sonnets to Karl Theodor German are among the most beautiful in German literature. Platen in the sonnet surpasses all the German poets, including even Goethe. In them perfection of form, and poignancy or wealth of emotion are

August von Platen

151

illustrated to perfection. The sentiment is similar to that of the sonnets of Shakespeare (with their personal note), and the form that of the Italian or French sonnet."

Platen, however, was unfortunate in his affairs of the heart, and there is a refrain of suffering in his poems which comes out characteristically in the following sonnet :—

Platen's Sonnets "SINCE pain is life and life is only pain,
Why he can feel what I have felt before,
Who seeing joy sees it again no more
The instant he attempts his joy to gain;
Who, caught as in a labyrinth unaware,
The outlet from it never more can find;
Whom love seems only for this end to bind—
In order to hand over to Despair;

Who prays each dizzy lightning-flash to end him,
Each star to reel his thread of life away
With all the torments which his heart are rending;
And envies even the dead their pillow of clay,
Where Love no more their foolish brains can steal.
He who knows this, knows me, and what I feel."

One of Platen's sonnets deals with an incident, referred to in an earlier page, namely, the death of

the poet Pindar in the theatre, in the arms of his
young friend Theoxenos:—

„OH! when I die, would I might fade away   *On the*
     Like the pale stars, swiftly and silently,   *Death of*
    Would that death's messenger might come to *Pindar*
      me,
As once it came to Pindar—so they say.
Not that I would in Life, or in my Verse,
   With him, the great Incomparable, compare;
   Only his Death, my friend, I ask to share:
But let me now the gracious tale rehearse.
Long at the play, hearing sweet Harmony,
   He sat; and wearied out at last, had lain
His cheek upon his dear one's comely knee;
   Then when it died away—the choral strain—
He who thus cushioned him said: Wake and come!
   But to the Gods above he had gone home."

THE correspondence of Richard Wagner discloses the existence of a very
warm friendship between him and
Ludwig II., the young king of Ba-
varia. Ludwig as a young man appears to have been
a very charming personality, good looking, engaging and sympathetic; everyone was fond of him.

Friendship

Yet his tastes led him away from "society," into retirement, and the companionship of Nature and a few chosen friends—often of humble birth. Already at the age of fifteen he had heard Lohengrin, and silently vowed to know the composer. One of his first acts when he came to the throne was to send for Wagner; and from the moment of their meeting a personal intimacy sprang up between them, which in due course led to the establishment of the theatre at Bayreuth, and to the liberation of Wagner's genius to the world. Though the young king at a later time lost his reason—probably owing to his over-sensitive emotional nature—this does not detract from the service that he rendered to Music by his generous attachment. How Wagner viewed the matter may be gathered from Wagner's letters.

Wagner and Ludwig II. "HE, the king, loves me, and with the deep feeling and glow of a first love; he perceives and knows everything about me, and understands me as my own soul. He wants me to stay with him always. . . . I am to be free and my own master, not his music-conductor—only my very self and his friend." *Letters to Mme. Eliza Wille*, 4th May, 1864.

"IT is true that I have my young king who genuinely adores me. You cannot form an idea of our relations. I recall one of the dreams of my youth. I once dreamed that Shakespeare was alive: that I really saw and spoke to him: I can never forget the impression that dream made on me. Then I would have wished to see Beethoven, though he was already dead. Something of the same kind must pass in the mind of this lovable man when with me. He says he can hardly believe that he really possesses me. None can read without astonishment, without enchantment, the letters he writes to me." *Ibid*, 9th Sept., 1864.

"I HOPE now for a long period to gain strength again by quiet work. This is made possible for me by the love of an unimaginably beautiful and thoughtful being: it seems that it *had* to be even so greatly gifted a man and one so destined for me, as this young King of Bavaria. What he is to me no one can imagine. My guardian! In his love I completely rest and fortify myself towards the completion of my task." *Letter to his brother-in-law*, 10th Sept., 1865.

[For letters from Ludwig to Wagner see Additions, infra p. 183.]

Friendship

IN these letters we see chiefly of course the passionate sentiments of which Ludwig was capable; but that Wagner fully understood the feeling and appreciated it may be gathered from various passages in his published writings—such as the following, in which he seeks to show how the devotion of comradeship became the chief formative influence of the Spartan State:—

Wagner on Greek Comradeship "THIS beauteous naked man is the kernel of all Spartanhood; from genuine delight in the beauty of the most perfect human body—that of the male—arose that spirit of comradeship which pervades and shapes the whole economy of the Spartan State. This love of man to man, in its primitive purity, proclaims itself as the noblest and least selfish utterance of man's sense of beauty, for it teaches man to sink and merge his entire self in the object of his affection;" and again:—"The higher element of that love of man to man consisted even in this: that it excluded the motive of egoistic physicalism. Nevertheless it not only included a purely spiritual bond of friendship, but this spiritual friendship was the blossom and the crown of the physical friendship. The latter sprang directly

156

from delight in the beauty, aye in the material bodily beauty of the beloved comrade; yet this delight was no egoistic yearning, but a thorough stepping out of self into unreserved sympathy with the comrade's joy in himself; involuntarily betrayed by his life-glad beauty-prompted bearing. This love, which had its basis in the noblest pleasures of both eye and soul—not like our modern postal correspondence of sober friendship, half business-like, half sentimental—was the Spartan's only tutoress of youth, the never-ageing instructress alike of boy and man, the ordainer of common feasts and valiant enterprises; nay the inspiring helpmeet on the battlefield. For this it was that knit the fellowship of love into battalions of war, and fore-wrote the tactics of death-daring, in rescue of the imperilled or vengeance for the slaughtered comrade, by the infrangible law of the soul's most natural necessity." *The Art-work of the Future, trans. by W. A. Ellis.*

E may close this record of celebrated Germans with the name of K. H. Ulrichs, a Hanoverian by birth who occupied for a long time an official position in the revenue department at Vienna, and who became well known about 1866 through his writings on the subject of friendship. He gives, in his pamphlet *Memnon*, an account of the "story of his heart" in early years. In an apparently quite natural way, and independently of outer influences, his thoughts had from the very first been of friends of his own sex. At the age of 14, the picture of a Greek hero or god, a statue, seen in a book woke in him the tenderest longings.

K. H.
Ulrichs "THIS picture (he says), put away from me, as it was, a hundred times, came again a hundred times before the eyes of my soul. But of course for the origin of my special temperament it is in no way responsible. It only woke up what was already slumbering there—a thing which might have been done equally well by something else."

From that time forward the boy worshipped with a kind of romantic devotion elder friends, young men in the prime of early manhood; and later still his writings threw a flood of light on the "urning" temperament—as he called it—of which he was himself so marked an example.

Some of Ulrich's verses are scattered among his prose writings :—

To his friend Eberhard.

"AND so farewell! perchance on Earth   *Ulrichs*
   God's finger—as 'twixt thee and me—   *Verses*
Will never make that wonder clear
   Why thus It drew me unto thee."

            Memnon, Leipzig, 1898, p. 104.

And this:—

"IT was the day of our first meeting—
   That happy day, in Davern's grove—
I felt the Spring wind's tender greeting,
   And April touched my heart to love.
Thy hand in mine lay kindly mated;
Thy gaze held mine quite fascinated—
   So gracious wast, and fair!
Thy glance my life-thread almost severed;
My heart for joy and gladness quivered,
   Nigh more than it could bear.

There in the grove at evening's hour
   The breeze thro' budding twigs hath ranged,
And lips have learned to meet each other,
   And kisses mute exchanged."

            Memnon, p. 23.

Friendship

G O return to England. With the beginning of the 19th century we find two great poets, Byron and Shelley, both interested in and even writing in a romantic strain on the subject in question.

Byron's attachment, when at Cambridge, to Eddleston the chorister, a youth two years younger than himself, is well known. In a youthful letter to Miss Pigot he, Byron, speaks of it in enthusiastic terms:

"Trin. Coll., Camb., *July* 5th, 1807.

Byron's Letters "I REJOICE to hear you are interested in my protégé; he has been my *almost constant* associate since October, 1805, when I entered Trinity College. His *voice* first attracted my attention, his *countenance* fixed it, and his *manners* attached me to him for ever. He departs for a mercantile house in town in October, and we shall probably not meet till the expiration of my minority, when I shall leave to his decision either entering as a partner through my interest or residing with me altogether. Of course he would in his present frame of mind prefer the latter, but he may alter his opinion previous to that period; however he shall have his choice. I certainly love him more than any human being, and neither time nor distance have had the

160

least effect on my (in general) changeable disposition. In short we shall put Lady E. Butler and Miss Ponsonby to the blush, Pylades and Orestes out of countenance, and want nothing but a catastrophe like Nisus and Euryalus to give Jonathan and David the 'go by.' He certainly is more attached to *me* than even I am in return. During the whole of my residence at Cambridge we met every day, summer and winter, without passing *one* tiresome moment, and separated each time with increasing reluctance."

Eddleston gave Byron a cornelian (brooch-pin) which Byron prized much, and is said to have kept all his life. He probably refers to it, and to the inequality of condition between him and Eddleston, in the following stanza from his poem, *The Adieu*, written about this time :—

"AND thou, my friend, whose gentle love   *The Adieu*
    Yet thrills my bosom's chords,
How much thy friendship was above
    Description's power of words!
Still near my breast thy gift I wear
Which sparkled once with Feeling's tear,
    Of Love, the pure, the sacred gem;
Our souls were equal, and our lot
In that dear moment quite forgot;
    Let pride alone condemn."

161

Friendship

HE Lady Eleanor Butler and Miss Sarah Ponsonby mentioned in the above letter were at that time living at Llangollen, in Wales, and were known as the "Ladies of Llangollen," their romantic attachment to each other having already become proverbial. When Miss Ponsonby was seventeen, and Lady E. Butler some twenty years older, they had run away from their respective and respectable homes in Ireland, and taking a cottage at Llangollen lived there, inseparable companions, for the rest of their lives. Letters and diaries of contemporary celebrities mention their romantic devotion. (The Duke of Wellington was among their visitors.) Lady Eleanor died in 1829, at the age of ninety; and Miss Ponsonby only survived her "beloved one" (as she always called her) by two years.

S to the allusion to Nisus and Euryalus, Byron's paraphrase of the episode (from the 9th book of Virgil's Æneid) serves to show his interest in it:—

"NISUS, the guardian of the portal, stood,   *Byron's*
    Eager to gild his arms with hostile blood; *Nisus and*
Well-skilled in fight the quivering lance to wield, *Euryalus*
Or pour his arrows thro' the embattled field:
From Ida torn, he left his Sylvan cave,
And sought a foreign home, a distant grave.
    To watch the movements of the Daunian host,
With him Euryalus sustains the post;
No lovelier mien adorn'd the ranks of Troy,
And beardless bloom yet graced the gallant boy;
Tho' few the seasons of his youthful life,
As yet a novice in the martial strife,
'Twas his, with beauty, valour's gifts to share—
A soul heroic, as his form was fair.
    These burn with one pure flame of generous
        love;
In peace, in war, united still they move;
Friendship and glory form their joint reward;
And now combined they hold their nightly guard."

[The two then carry out a daring raid on the
enemy, in which Euryalus is slain. Nisus, coming to
his rescue is—after performing prodigies of valor—
slain too.]

"Thus Nisus all his fond affection proved—
Dying, revenged the fate of him he loved;

Friendship

Then on his bosom sought his wonted place,
And death was heavenly in his friend's embrace!
  Celestial pair! if aught my verse can claim,
Wafted on Time's broad pinion, yours is fame!
Ages on ages shall your fate admire,
No future day shall see your names expire,
While stands the Capitol, immortal dome!
And vanquished millions hail their empress,
  Rome!"

Byron's friendships, in fact, with young men were so marked that Moore in his *Life and Letters of Lord Byron* seems to have felt it necessary to mention and, to some extent, to explain them:—

T. Moore on Byron
"DURING his stay in Greece (in 1810) we find him forming one of those extraordinary friendships—if attachment to persons so inferior to himself can be called by that name—of which I have already mentioned two or three instances in his younger days, and in which the pride of being a protector and the pleasure of exciting gratitude seem to have contributed to his mind the chief, pervading charm. The person whom he now adopted in this manner, and from similar feelings to those which had inspired his early attachments to the cottage boy near Newstead and the young chorister at Cambridge, was a Greek youth, named

164

Nicolo Giraud, the son, I believe, of a widow lady in whose house the artist Lusieri lodged. In this young man he seems to have taken the most lively and even brotherly interest."

SHELLEY, in his fragmentary *Essay on Friendship*—stated by his friend Hogg to have been written "not long before his death"—says:—

"I REMEMBER forming an attachment of this *Shelley on* kind at school. I cannot recall to my memory *Friendship* the precise epoch at which this took place; but I imagine it must have been at the age of eleven or twelve. The object of these sentiments was a boy about my own age, of a character eminently gener-ous, brave and gentle, and the elements of human feeling seemed to have been, from his birth, geni-ally compounded within him. There was a delicacy and a simplicity in his manners, inexpressibly attrac-tive. It has never been my fortune to meet with him since my schoolboy days; but either I con-found my present recollections with the delusions of past feelings, or he is now a source of honour and utility to everyone around him. The tones of his voice were so soft and winning, that every word pierced into my heart; and their pathos was so deep that in listening to him the tears have in-

165

voluntarily gushed from my eyes. Such was the being for whom I first experienced the sacred sentiments of friendship."

It may be noted that Hogg takes the reference as to himself !

WITH this passage we may compare the following from Leigh Hunt :—

"IF I had reaped no other benefit from Christ Hospital, the school would be ever dear to me from the recollection of the friendships I formed in it, and of the first heavenly taste it gave me of that most spiritual of the affections. . . . If ever I tasted a disembodied transport on earth, it was in those friendships which I entertained at school, before I dreamt of any maturer feeling. I shall never forget the impression it made on me. I loved my friend for his gentleness, his candour, his truth, his good repute, his freedom even from my own livelier manner, his calm and reasonable kindness. It was not any particular talent that attracted me to him, or anything striking whatsoever. I should say, in one word, it was his goodness. I doubt whether he ever had a conception of a tithe of the regard and respect I entertained for him ; and I smile to think of the perplexity (though he never showed it) which he probably felt sometimes at my enthusiastic expressions; for I thought him a kind of angel. It is no exaggeration to say, that, take away the unspiritual part of it—the genius and the knowledge—and there is no height of conceit indulged in by the most romantic character in Shakespeare, which surpassed what I felt towards the merits I ascribed to him, and the delight which I took in his society. With the other boys I played antics, and rioted in fantastic jests; but in his society, or whenever I thought of him, I fell into a kind of Sabbath state of bliss; and I am sure I could have died for him.

"I experienced this delightful affection towards three successive schoolfellows, till two of them had for some time gone out into the world and forgotten me; but it grew less with each, and in more than one instance became rivalled by a new set of emotions, especially in regard to the last, for I fell in love with his sister—at least, I thought so. But on the occurrence of her death, not long after, I was startled at finding myself assume an air of greater sorrow than I felt, and at being willing to be relieved by the sight of the first pretty face that turned towards me. . . . My friend, who died himself not long after his quitting the University, was of a German family in the service of the court, very

167

refined and musical." *Autobiography of Leigh Hunt, Smith and Elder,* 1870, p. 75.

N this subject of boy-friendships and their intensity Lord Beaconsfield has, in *Coningsby,* a quite romantic passage, which notwithstanding its sentimental setting may be worth quoting; because, after all, it signalises an often-forgotten or unconsidered aspect of school-life :—

Lord "AT school, friendship is a passion. It entrances
Beacons- the being; it tears the soul. All loves of after-
field's life can never bring its rapture, or its wretched-
"Con- ness; no bliss so absorbing, no pangs of jealousy
ingsby" or despair so crushing and so keen! What tenderness and what devotion; what illimitable confidence, infinite revelations of inmost thoughts; what ecstatic present and romantic future; what bitter estrangements and what melting reconciliations; what scenes of wild recrimination, agitating explanations, passionate correspondence; what insane sensitiveness, and what frantic sensibility; what earthquakes of the heart and whirlwinds of the soul are confined in that simple phrase, a schoolboy's friendship!"

LFRED TENNYSON, in his great poem *In Memoriam*, published about the middle of the 19th century, gives superb expression to his love for his lost friend, Arthur Hallam. Reserved, dignified, in sustained meditation and tender sentiment, yet half revealing here and there a more passionate feeling; expressing in simplest words the most difficult and elusive thoughts (*e.g.*, Cantos 128 and 129), as well as the most intimate and sacred moods of the soul; it is indeed a great work of art. Naturally, being such, it was roundly abused by the critics on its first appearance. The *Times* solemnly rebuked its language as unfitted for any but amatory tenderness, and because young Hallam was a barrister spent much wit upon the poet's "Amaryllis of the Chancery bar." Tennyson himself, speaking of *In Memoriam*, mentioned (see *Memoir* by his son, p. 800) "the number of shameful letters of abuse he had received about it!"

Friendship

CANTO XIII.

Tennyson's "In Memoriam"

"TEARS of the widower, when he sees,
  A late-lost form that sleep reveals,
  And moves his doubtful arms, and feels
Her place is empty, fall like these;

Which weep a loss for ever new,
  A void where heart on heart reposed;
  And, where warm hands have prest and closed,
Silence, till I be silent too.

Which weep the comrade of my choice,
  An awful thought, a life removed,
  The human-hearted man I loved,
A spirit, not a breathing voice.

Come Time, and teach me, many years,
  I do not suffer in a dream;
  For now so strange do these things seem,
Mine eyes have leisure for their tears;

My fancies time to rise on wing,
  And glance about the approaching sails,
  As tho' they brought but merchant's bales,
And not the burden that they bring."

170

Canto XVIII.

"'TIS well, 'tis something, we may stand
    Where he in English earth is laid,
    And from his ashes may be made
The violet of his native land.

'Tis little; but it looks in truth
    As if the quiet bones were blest
    Among familiar names to rest
And in the places of his youth.

Come then, pure hands, and bear the head
    That sleeps, or wears the mask of sleep,
    And come, whatever loves to weep,
And hear the ritual of the dead.

Ah yet, ev'n yet, if this might be,
    I, falling on his faithful heart,
    Would breathing thro' his lips impart
The life that almost dies in me:

That dies not, but endures with pain,
    And slowly forms the firmer mind,
    Treasuring the look it cannot find,
The words that are not heard again."

Friendship

Canto LIX.

"In Memoriam"

"IF, in thy second state sublime,
  Thy ransom'd reason change replies
  With all the circle of the wise,
The perfect flower of human time;

And if thou cast thine eyes below,
  How dimly character'd and slight,
  How dwarf'd a growth of cold and night
How blanch'd with darkness must I grow!

Yet turn thee to the doubtful shore,
  Where thy first form was made a man;
  I loved thee, Spirit, and love, nor can
The soul of Shakspeare love thee more."

Canto CXXVII.

"DEAR friend, far off, my lost desire,
  So far, so near, in woe or weal;
  O loved the most when most I feel
There is a lower and a higher;

Known and unknown, human, divine!
  Sweet human hand and lips and eye,
  Dear heavenly friend that canst not die,
Mine, mine, for ever, ever, mine!

172

Strange friend, past, present and to be;
   Loved deeplier, darklier understood;
   Behold I dream a dream of good
And mingle all the world with thee."

Canto CXXVIII.

"THY voice is on the rolling air;
   I hear thee where the waters run;
   Thou standest in the rising sun,
And in the setting thou art fair.

What art thou then? I cannot guess;
   But tho' I seem in star and flower
   To feel thee some diffusive power,
I do not therefore love thee less:

My love involves the love before;
   My love is vaster passion now;
   Tho' mixed with God and Nature thou,
I seem to love thee more and more.

Far off thou art, but ever nigh;
   I have thee still, and I rejoice;
   I prosper, circled with thy voice;
I shall not lose thee tho' I die."

173

Friendship

OLLOWING is a little poem by
Robert Browning entitled *May and
Death*, which may well be placed near
the stanzas of *In Memoriam* :—

*Brown-
ing's
May and
Death'*
"I WISH that when you died last May,
   Charles, there had died along with you
Three parts of Spring's delightful things;
   Ay, and for me the fourth part too.

A foolish thought, and worse, perhaps!
   There must be many a pair of friends
Who arm-in-arm deserve the warm
   Moon-births and the long evening-ends.

So, for their sake, be May still May!
   Let their new time, as mine of old,
Do all it did for me; I bid
   Sweet sights and sounds throng manifold.

Only one little sight, one plant
   Woods have in May, that starts up green
Save a sole streak which, so to speak,
   Is Spring's blood, spilt its leaves between—

That, they might spare; a certain wood
   Might miss the plant; their loss were small;
But I—whene'er the leaf grows there—
   It's drop comes from my heart, that's all."

174

ETWEEN Browning and Whitman we may insert a few lines from R. W. Emerson:—

"THE only way to have a friend *Ralph* is to be one. . . . In the last *Waldo* analysis love is only the reflection of a man's own *Emerson* worthiness from other men. Men have sometimes exchanged names with their friends, as if they would signify that in their friend each loved his own soul.

"The higher the style we demand of friendship, of course the less easy to establish it with flesh and blood. . . . Friends, such as we desire, are dreams and fables. But a sublime hope cheers ever the faithful heart, that elsewhere, in other regions of the universal power, souls are now acting, enduring, and daring, which can love us, and which we can love." *Essay on Friendship.*

These also from Henry D. Thoreau:—

'NO word is oftener on the lips of men than Friendship, and indeed no thought is more *Henry D* familiar to their aspirations. All men are dreaming *Thoreau* of it, and its drama, which is always a tragedy, is enacted daily. It is the secret of the universe. You may thread the town, you may wander the country, and none shall ever speak of it, yet thought is everywhere busy about it, and the idea of what is possible in this respect affects our behaviour towards all new men and women, and a great many old ones. Nevertheless I can remember only two or three essays on this subject in all literature. . . . To say that a man is your friend, means commonly no more than this, that he is not your enemy. Most contemplate only what would be the accidental and trifling advantages of friendship, as that the friend can assist in time of need, by his substance, or his influence, or his counsel; but he who foresees such advantages in this relation proves himself blind to its real advantage, or indeed wholly inexperienced in the relation itself. . . . What is commonly called Friendship is only a little more honour among rogues. But sometimes we are said to *love* another, that is, to stand in a true relation to him, so that we give the best to, and receive the best from, him. Between whom there is hearty truth there is love; and in proportion to our truthfulness and confidence in one another our lives are divine and miraculous, and answer to our ideal. There are passages of affection in our intercourse with mortal men and women, such as no prophecy had taught us to expect, which transcend our earthly life, and anticipate heaven for us." *From On the Concord River.*

Renaissance & Modern Times

I CONCLUDE this collection with a few quotations from Whitman, for whom "the love of comrades" perhaps stands as the most intimate part of his message to the world—"Here the frailest leaves of me and yet my strongest lasting." Whitman, by his great power, originality and initiative, as well as by his deep insight and wide vision, is in many ways the inaugurator of a new era to mankind; and it is especially interesting to find that this idea of comradeship, and of its establishment as a *social institution*, plays so important a part with him. We have seen that in the Greek age, and more or less generally in the ancient and pagan world, comradeship was an institution; we have seen that in Christian and modern times, though existent, it was socially denied and ignored, and indeed to a great extent fell under a kind of ban; and now Whitman's attitude towards it suggests to us that it really is destined to pass into its third stage, to arise again, and become a recognised factor of modern life, and

Friendship

even in a more extended and perfect form than at first.[a]

Walt "IT is to the development, identification, and
Whitman general prevalence of that fervid comradeship
(the adhesive love, at least rivaling the amative
love hitherto possessing imaginative literature, if
not going beyond it), that I look for the counter-
balance and offset of our materialistic and vulgar
American Democracy, and for the spiritualisation
thereof. Many will say it is a dream, and will not
follow my inferences; but I confidently expect a
time when there will be seen, running like a half-
hid warp through all the myriad audible and visible worldly interests of America, threads of manly
friendship, fond and loving, pure and sweet, strong
and lifelong, carried to degrees hitherto unknown
—not only giving tone to individual character, and
making it unprecedently emotional, muscular, heroic, and refined, but having deepest relations to
general politics. I say Democracy infers such
loving comradeship, as its most inevitable twin or

[a] As Whitman in this connection (like Tennyson in connection with
In Memoriam) is sure to be accused of morbidity, it may be worth while
to insert the following note from *In re Walt* Whitman, p. 115, "Dr.
Drinkard in 1870, when Whitman broke down from rupture of a small
blood-vessel in the brain, wrote to a Philadelphia doctor detailing
Whitman's case, and stating that he was a man 'with the most natural
habits, bases, and organisation he had ever seen.' "

counterpart, without which it will be incomplete, in vain, and incapable of perpetuating itself."
Democratic Vistas, note.

The three following poems are taken from *Leaves of Grass :--*

"RECORDERS ages hence,　　　　　　　"*Leaves of*
　　Come, I will take you down underneath this *Grass*"
　　　impassive exterior, I will tell you what to
　　　say of me,
Publish my name and hang up my picture as that
　　of the tenderest lover,
The friend the lover's portrait, of whom his friend
　　his lover was fondest,
Who was not proud of his songs, but of the mea-
　　sureless ocean of love within him, and freely
　　pour'd it forth,
Who often walk'd lonesome walks thinking of his
　　dear friends, his lovers,
Who pensive away from one he lov'd often lay
　　sleepless and dissatisfied at night,
Who knew too well the sick, sick dread lest the one
　　he lov'd might secretly be indifferent to him,
Whose happiest days were far away through fields,
　　in woods, on hills, he and another wandering
　　hand in hand, they twain apart from other men,

179

Friendship

Who oft as he saunter'd the streets curv'd with his
   arm the shoulder of his friend, while the arm of
   his friend rested upon him also."

             Leaves of Grass, 1891-2 edn., p. 102.

"WHEN I heard at the close of the day how
      my name had been receiv'd with plaudits
   in the capitol, still it was not a happy night for
   me that follow'd,
And else when I carous'd, or when my plans were
   accomplish'd, still I was not happy,
But the day when I rose at dawn from the bed of
   perfect health, refresh'd, singing, inhaling the
   ripe breath of autumn,
When I saw the full moon in the west grow pale
   and disappear in the morning light,
When I wander'd alone over the beach, and un-
   dressing bathed, laughing with the cool waters,
   and saw the sun rise,
And when I thought how my dear friend my lover
   was on his way coming, O then I was happy,
O then each breath tasted sweeter, and all that day
   my food nourish'd me more, and the beautiful
   day pass'd well,
And the next came with equal joy, and with the
   next at evening came my friend,

And that night while all was still I heard the waters
    roll slowly continuously up the shores,
I heard the hissing rustle of the liquid and sands as
    directed to me whispering to congratulate me,
For the one I love most lay sleeping by me under
    the same cover in the cool night,
In the stillness in the autumn moonbeams his face
    was inclined toward me,
And his arm lay lightly around my breast—and
    that night I was happy."

Ibid, p. 103.

"I HEAR it was charged against me that I sought
    to destroy institutions,
But really I am neither for nor against institutions,
(What indeed have I in common with them? or
    what with the destruction of them?)
Only I will establish in the Mannahatta and in
    every city of these States inland and seaboard,
And in the fields and woods, and above every keel
    little or large that dents the water,
Without edifices or rules or trustees or any argu-
    ment,
The institution of the dear love of comrades."

Ibid, p. 107.

Additions
[1906]

Greek Times

ARISTOTLE (Ethics bk. viii.) says: "FRIENDSHIP is a thing most *Aristotle* necessary to life, since without friends no one would choose to live, though possessed of all other advantages." . . . . "Since then his own life is, to a good man, a thing naturally sweet and ultimately desirable, for a similar reason is the life of his friend agreeable to him, and delightful merely on its own account, and without reference to any object beyond it ; and to live without friends is to be destitute of a good, unconditioned, absolute, and in itself desirable ; and therefore to be deprived of one of the most solid and most substantial of all enjoyments."

"Being asked 'What is Friendship ?' Aristotle replied 'One soul in two bodies.'" *Diog. Laertius.*

EPAMINONDAS and Pelopidas, the Theban statesmen and generals, were celebrated for their devotion to each other. In a battle (B.C. 385) against the Arcadians, Epaminondas is said to have saved

185

his friend's life.   Plutarch in his Life of Pelopidas
relates of them :—

Epamin- "E PAMINONDAS and he were both born
ondas and   with the same dispositions to all kinds of
Pelopidas virtues, but Pelopidas took more pleasure in the
exercises of the body, and Epaminondas in the
improvements of the mind ; so that they spent
all their leisure time, the one in hunting, and
the palestra, the other in learned conversation,
and the study of philosophy. But of all the
famous actions for which they are so much celebrated, the judicious part of mankind reckon
none so great and glorious as that strict friendship
which they inviolably preserved through the
whole course of their lives, in all the high posts
they held, both military and civil. . . . For
being both in that battle, near one another in the
infantry, and fighting against the Arcadians, that
wing of the Lacedæmonians in which they were,
gave way and was broken ; which Pelopidas and
Epaminondas perceiving, they joined their shields,
and keeping close together, bravely repulsed all
that attacked them, till at last Pelopidas, after
receiving seven large wounds, fell upon a heap
of friends and enemies that lay dead together.
Epaminondas, though he believed him slain, ad-

vanced before him to defend his body and arms, and for a long time maintained his ground against great numbers of the Arcadians, being resolved to die rather than desert his companion and leave him in the enemy's power ; but being wounded in his breast by a spear, and in his arm by a sword, he was quite disabled and ready to fall, when Agesipolis, king of the Spartans, came from the other wing to his relief, and beyond all expectation saved both their lives."

POLEMON and Krates were followers of Plato in philosophy, and in their time (about 300 B.C.) leaders of the Platonic School. They were, according to Hesychius, devoted friends :

"KRATES and Polemon loved each other so *Polemon* well that they not only were occupied in *and* life with the same work, but they almost drew *Krates* breath simultaneously ; and in death they shared the same grave. On account of which, Archesilaus, who visited them in company with Theophrastus (a pupil of Aristotle), spoke of them as gods, or survivors from the Golden Age."

Hesychius **xl.**

ALEXANDER, the great World-Conqueror, was born B.C. 356, and was King of Macedonia B.C. 336-323. His great favorite was Hephæstion, who had been brought up and educated with him.

Alexander and Hephæstion

"WHEN Hephæstion died (at Ecbatana in 324) Alexander placed his weapons upon the funeral pyre, with gold and silver for the dead man, and a robe—which last, among the Persians is a symbol of great honour. He shore off his own hair, as in Homeric grief, and behaved like the Achilles of Homer. Indeed he acted more violently and passionately than the latter, for he caused the towers and strongholds of Ecbatana to be demolished all round. As long as he only dedicated his own hair, he was behaving, I think, like a Greek ; but when he laid hands on the very walls, Alexander was already showing his grief in foreign fashion. Even in his clothing he departed from ordinary custom, and gave himself up to his mood, his love, and his tears."

Aelian's Varia Historia, vii, 8.

Persian Poetry

VON Kupffer, in his Anthology, *Lieblingminne und Freundes liebe in der Weltliteratur*, gives the following three poems from Sadi and Hafiz:—

"A YOUTH there was of golden heart and nature,
Who loved a friend, his like in every feature;
Once, as upon the ocean sailed the pair,
They chanced into a whirlpool unaware.
A fisherman made haste the first to save,
Ere his young life should meet a watery grave;
But crying from the raging surf, he said:
'Leave me, and seize my comrade's hand instead.'
E'en as he spoke the mortal swoon o'ertook him,
With that last utterance life and sense forsook
   him.

Learn not love's temper from that shallow pate
Who in the hour of fear forsakes his mate;
True friends will ever act like him above
(Trust one who is experienced in love);
For Sadi knows full well the lover's part,
And Bagdad understands the Arab heart.
More than all else thy loved one shalt thou prize,
Else is the whole world hidden from thine eyes."

From Sadi's Rose Garden

189

From
Sadi's
Pleasure
Garden

"LOV'ST thou a being formed of dust like
thee—
Peace and contentment from thy heart shall flee ;
Waking, fair limbs and features shall torment
thee ;
Sleeping, thy love in dreams shall hold and haunt
thee.
Under his feet thy head is bowed to earth ;
Compared with him the world's a paltry crust ;
If to thy loved one gold is nothing worth,
Why, then to thee is gold no more than dust.
Hardly a word for others canst thou find,
For no room's left for others in thy mind."

Hafiz
to his
Friend

"DEAR Friend, since thou hast passed the
whole
Of one sweet night, till dawn, with me,
I were scarce mortal, could I spend
Another hour apart from thee.
The fear of death, for all of time
Hath left me since my soul partook
The water of true Life, that wells
In sweet abundance from thy brook."

Renaissance

BEAUMONT and Fletcher are two names which time and immortal friendship have sealed in one. Francis Beaumont was son of a judge, and John Fletcher, who was some four or five years the elder of the two, son of a bishop. The one went to Oxford, the other to Cambridge. Both took to writing at an early age; they probably met at the Mermaid Tavern, about the year 1604, and a friendship sprang up between them of the closest character. "The intimacy which now commenced was one of singular warmth even for that romantic age." (Chambers' Biog. Dict.) For many years they lived in the same house as bachelors, writing plays together, and sharing everything in common. Then in 1613 Beaumont married, but died in 1616. Fletcher lived on unmarried, till 1625, when he died of the plague.

J. St. L. Strachey, in his introduction to the works of Beaumont and Fletcher in the Mermaid Series, says :—

Beaumont "IN the whole range of English literature, search
and it from Chaucer till to-day, there is no figure
Fletcher more fascinating or more worthy of attention
than 'the mysterious double personallity' of Beaumont and Fletcher. Whether we bow to the
sentiment of the first Editor, who, though he
knew the secret of the poets, yet since never
parted while they lived' conceived it not equitable
to 'separate their ashes,' and so refuse to think
of them apart ; whether we adopt the legendary
union of the comrade-poets who dwelt on the
Bank-side, who lived and worked together, their
thoughts no less in common than the cloak and
bed o'er which tradition has grown fond ; whether
we think of them as two minds so married that
to divorce or disunite them were a sacrilegious
deed ; or whether we yield to the subtler influences of the critical fancy, and delight to
discover and explore each from its source, the
twin fountains of inspiration that feed the majestic
stream of song that flows through 'The Lost
Aspatia's' tragedy, etc. . . . whether we treat
the poets as a mystery to which love and sympathy are the initiation, or as a problem for the
tests and reagents of critical analysis to solve,
the double name of Beaumont and Fletcher will

ever strike the fancy and excite the imagination as does no other name in the annals of English song."

George Varley, in his Introduction to the works of B. and F. (London, E. Moxon, 1839) says :—

"THE story of their common life, which scandalises some biographers, contains much that is agreeable to me, as offering a picture of perfect union whose heartiness excuses its homeliness . . . but when critics would explain away the community of cloak and clothes by accident or slander, methinks their fastidiousness exceeds their good feeling."

Beaumont was a man of great personal beauty and charm. Ben Jonson was much attracted to him. Fletcher delighted to do him honour and to put his name first on their title page ; though it is probable that Beaumont's share in the plays was the lesser one. See following verses by Sir Aston Cokaine in the 1st Collection of their works, published 1647 :—

193   ☛ SHEET FOURTEEN

Sweet
Fletcher's
Brain

"IN the large book of playes you late did print,
In Beaumont and in Fletcher's name, why in't
Did you not justice?   Give to each his due?
For Beaumont of those many writ in few,
And Massinger in other few; the main
Being sole issues of sweet Fletcher's brain.
But how came I, you ask, so much to know?
Fletcher's chief bosome-friend inform'd me so. '

The following lines were written by Fletcher
on the death of Beaumont :—

Fletcher's
lament for
his Friend

"COME, sorrow, come! bring all thy cries,
All thy laments, and all thy weeping eyes!
Burn out, you living monuments of woe!
Sad, sullen griefs, now rise and overflow!
                Virtue is dead;
                Oh! cruel fate!
                All youth is fled;
                All our laments too late.
Oh, noble youth, to thy ne'er dying name,
Oh, happy youth, to thy still growing fame,
To thy long peace in earth, this sacred knell
Our last loves ring—farewell, farewell, farewell!
Go, happy soul, to thy eternal birth!
And press his body lightly, gentle Earth.'

194

Renaissance

And among the poems attributed to Francis Beaumont is one generally supposed to be addressed to Fletcher, and speaking of an alliance hidden from the world—of which the last five lines run :—

"IF when I die, physicians doubt
What caused my death, and these to view
Of all their judgments, which was true,
Rip up my heart ; O, then I fear
The world will see thy picture there."

An Epitaph

—though it is perhaps more probable that it was addressed to Beaumont by Fletcher, and has accidentally found place among the former's writings.

In the *Maid's Tragedy* by B. and F., (Act I. Scene i.) we have Melantius speaking about his companion Amintor, a young nobleman :—

"ALL joys upon him ! for he is my friend.
Wonder not that I call a man so young my
friend :
His worth is great ; radiant he is, and temperate ;
And one that never thinks his life his own,
If his friend need it "

HE devotion of Vauvenargues to his friend De Seytres is immortalized by the *éloge* he wrote on the occasion of the latter's death. V., a youth of noble family, born in S. France in 1715, entered military service and the regiment of the King at an early age. He seems to have been a gentle, wise character, much beloved by his comrades. During the French invasion of Bohemia, in 1741, when he was about 26, he met Hippolyte de Seytres, who belonged to the same regiment, and who was only 18 years of age. A warm friendship sprang up between the two, but lasted for a brief time only. De Seytres died during the privations of the terrible Siege of Prague in 1742. Vauvenargues escaped, but with the loss of his health, as well as of his friend. He took to literature, and wrote some philosophic works, and became correspondent and friend of Voltaire, but died in 1747 at the early age of 32. In his *éloge* he speaks of his friend as follows :—

Modern Times

'BY nature full of grace, his movements natural, Vauvenar- his manners frank, his features noble and gues on grave, his expression sweet and penetrating ; one De Seytres could not look upon him with indifference. From the first his loveable exterior won all hearts in his favour, and whoever was in the position to know his character could not but admire the beauty of his disposition. Never did he despise or envy or hate anyone. He understood all the passions and opinions, even the most singular, that the world blames. They did not surprise him ; he penetrated their cause, and found in his own reflexions the means of explaining them."

"And so Hippolyte," he continues, "I was destined to be the survivor in our friendship—just when I was hoping that it would mitigate all the sufferings and ennui of my life even to my latest breath. At the moment when my heart, full of security, placed blind confidence in thy strength and youth, and abandoned itself to gladness—O Misery ! in that moment a mighty hand was extinguishing the sources of life in thy blood. Death was creeping into thy heart, and harbouring in thy bosom ! . . . O pardon me once more ; for never canst thou have doubted the depth of my attachment. I loved thee before I was able to know thee. I have never loved but thee . . . I was ignorant of thy very name and life, but my heart adored thee, spoke with thee, saw thee and sought thee in solitude. Thou knewest me but for a moment ; and when we did become acquainted, already a thousand times had I paid homage in secret to thy virtues. . . . Shade worthy of heaven, whither hast thou fled ! Do my sighs reach thee ? I tremble —O abyss profound, O woe, O death, O grave ! Dark veil and viewless night, and mystery of Eternity ! "

(It is said that Vauvenargues thought more of this memorial inscription to his friend than of any other of his works, and constantly worked at and perfected it.)

CHILLER, the great German poet, had an enthusiastic appreciation of friendship-love, as can be seen from his poems "Freundschaft" and "Die Burgschaft," and others of his writings. His tragedy Don Karlos turns upon the

death of one friend for the sake of another. The
young Infanta of Spain, Don Karlos, alienated by
the severities of his father, Phillip II., enters into
plots and intrigues, from the consequences of
which he is only saved by his devoted companion,
the Marquis of Posa, who, by making himself out
the guilty party, dies in the Prince's stead. Early
in the play (Act I., Scene ii.) the attachment
between the two is outlined :—

Karlos. Oh, if indeed 'tis true— *From*
    What my heart says—that out of millions, *Schiller's*
        thou   *Don*
    Hast been decreed at last to understand me ; *Karlos*
    If it be true that Nature all-creative
    In moulding Karlos copied Roderick,
    And strung the tender chords of our two souls
    Harmonious in the morning of our lives ;
    If even a tear that eases thus my sorrow
    Is dearer to thee than my father's favour—

Marquis of Posa. Oh, dearer than the world !

Karlos. So low, so low
    Have I now fallen, have become so needy,
    That of our early childish years together

Karlos
and
Roderick

I must remind thee—must indeed entreat
Thy payment of those long-forgotten debts
Which thou, while yet in sailor garb, con-
    tractedst ;
When thou and I, two boys of venturous
    habit,
Grew up, and side by side, in brotherhood.
No grief oppressed me then—save that thy
    spirit
Seemed so eclipsing mine—until at length
I boldly dared to *love* thee without limit,
Since to be *like* thee was beyond my dreams.
Then I began, with myriad tenderness
And brother-love most loyal, to torment thee ;
And thou, proud heart, returned it all so
    coldly.
Oft would I stand there—and thou saw'st it
    not !
And hot and heavy tear-drops from my eyes
Hung, when perchance, thou, Roderick,
    hastening past me,
Would'st throw thy arms about some lesser
    playmate.
"Why only these?" I cried, and wept aloud
"Am I not also worthy of thy heart ?"
But thou—

So cold and serious before me kneeling,
"Homage" thou said'st, "to the King's son
    is due."

Marquis.   A truce, O Prince, to all these tales
    of childhood,
They make my cheeks red even now with
    shame !

Karlos.   And this from thee indeed I did not
    merit.
Contemn thou could'st, and even rend my
    heart,
But ne'er estrange.   Three times thou did'st
    repulse
The young Prince from thee ; thrice again
    he came
As suppliant to thee—to entreat thy love,
And urgently to press his love upon thee.
But that which Karlos could not, chance
    effected.

(The story is then related of how as a boy he
took on himself the blame for a misdemeanour of
Roderick's, and was severely punished by his
royal father)—

Under the pitiless strokes my blood flowed
    red ;
I looked on thee and wept not. But the King
Was angered by my boyish heroism,
And for twelve terrible hours emprisoned me
In a dark dungeon, to repent thereof.
So proud and fierce was my determination
By Roderick to be beloved. Thou cam'st
And loudly weeping at my feet did'st fall,
"Yes, yes," did'st cry, "my pride is over-
    come,
One day, when thou art king, I will repay
    thee."

Marquis (giving his hand.)
I will so, Karl. My boyish affidavit
As man I now renew ; I will repay ;
My hour will also strike, perchance.

(The hour comes, when Roderick takes on
himself the blame for an intrigue of Don Karlos
with the Queen and William of Orange. He
writes a letter to the latter, and allows it purposely
to fall into the King's hands. He is assassinated
by order of the King ; and the following speech
over his body (Act V., Scene iv.) is made to the

King by Don Karlos, who thenceforth abjures all
love except for the memory of his friend.)

Karlos (to the King.)   *The*
    The dead man was my friend.   And would *devotion*
      you know   *of*
    Wherefore he died ?   He perished for my *Roderick*
      sake.
    Yes, Sire, for we were brothers ! brothers by
    A nobler chain than Nature ever forges.
    Love was his glorious life-career.   And love
    For me, his great, his glorious death.   Mine
      was he.
    What time his lowly bearing puffed you up,
    What time his gay persuasive eloquence
    Made easy sport of your proud giant-spirit.
    You thought to dominate him quite—and
      were
    The obedient creature of his deeper plans.
    That I am prisoner, is the schemed result
    Of his great friendship.   To achieve my safety
    He wrote that letter to the Prince of Orange—
    O God ! the first, last falsehood of his life.
    To rescue me he went to meet the Fate
    Which he has suffered.   With your gracious
      favours

You loaded him. He died for me. On
    him
You pressed the favours of your heart and
    friendship.
Your sceptre was the plaything of his hands ;
He threw it from him, and for me he died.

THERE is little, I believe, in the historical facts relating to Don Karlos to justify this tale of friendship ; but there seems great probability that the incidents were transferred by Schiller from the history of Frederick the Great, of Prussia, when a youth at his father's court. The devotion that existed between the young Frederick and Lieut. Von Katte, the anger and severities of the royal parent, the supposed conspiracy, the emprisonment of Frederick, and the execution of Von Katte, are all reproduced in Schiller's play.

Fritz of Prussia and Von Katte Von Katte was a young man of good family and strange but charming personality, who, as soon as he came to Court, being three or four years older than Frederick, exercised a strong attraction upon the latter. The two were always together, and finally, enraged by the harshness of the royal father, they plotted flight to England. They were arrested, and Katte, accused of treason to the throne, was condemned to death. That this sentence was pronounced, not so much for political reasons, as in order to do despite to the affection between him and the Crown Prince, is strongly suggested by the circumstances. Von Katte was sent from a distance in order to be executed at Cüstrin, in the fortress where the Prince was confined, and with instructions that the latter should witness his execution. Carlyle, in his life of Frederick II., says :—

"KATTE wore, by order, a brown dress exactly *Death of* like the Prince's ; the Prince is already *Von Katte* brought down into a lower room to see Katte as he passes, (to see Katte die has been the royal order, but they smuggled that into abeyance) and Katte knows he shall see him." [Besserer, the chaplain of the Garrison, quoted by Carlyle, describing the scene as they approached the Castle, says :—'Here, after long wistful looking about, he did get sight of his beloved Jonathan at a window in the Castle, from whom, he, with politest and most tender expression, speaking in French, took leave, with no little emotion of sorrow.] "*Pardonnez moi, mon cher Katte*" cried Friedrich. "*La mort est douce pour un si aimable Prince*," said Katte, and fared on ; round some angle of the Fortress it appears ; not in sight of Friedrich, who sank in a faint, and had seen his last glimpse of Katte in this world."

Life of Frederick II., vol. 2, p. 489.

Frederick the Great Frederick's grief and despair were extreme for a time. Then his royal father found him a wife, in the Princess Elizabeth of Brunswick, whom he obediently married, but in whom he showed little interest—their meetings growing rarer and rarer till at last they became merely formal. Later, and after his accession, he spent most of his leisure time when away from the cares of war and political re-organisation, at his retreat at Sans-Souci, afar from feminine society (a fact which provoked Voltaire's sarcasms), and in the society of his philosophic and military friends, to many of whom he was much attached. Von Kupffer has unearthed from his poems printed at Sans-Souci in 1750 the following, addressed to Count Von Kaiserlinck, a favorite companion, on whom he bestowed the by-name of Cesarion :—

"CESARION, let us keep unspoiled
    Our faith, and be true friends,
And pair our lives like noble Greeks,
        And to like noble ends !
That friend from friend may never hide
A fault through weakness or thro' pride,
        Or sentiment that cloys.
Thus gold in fire the brighter glows,
And far more rare and precious grows,
        Refined from all alloys."

There is also in the same collection a long and beautiful ode "To the shades of Cesarion," of which the following are a few lines :—

"O GOD ! how hard the word of Fate !
    Cesarion dead !   His happy days
Death to the grave has consecrate.
        His charm I mourn and gentle grace.
He's dead—my tender, faithful mate !

*Frederick
to
Cesarion*

207

A thousand daggers pierce my heart ;
It trembles, torn with grief and pain.
    He's gone ! the dawn comes not again !
Thy grave's the goal of my heart's strife ;
    Holy shall thy remembrance be ;
To thee I poured out love in life ;
    And love in death I vow to thee."

JOHANN Gottfried von Herder (1744-1803) as theologian, philosopher, friend of Goethe, Court preacher at Weimar, and author of *Ideas on the Philosophy of History* has had a great and enduring reputation. The following extract is from the just-mentioned book :—

Herder on Greek Friendship "NEVER has a branch born finer fruit than that little branch of Olive, Ivy, and Pine, which was the victor's crown among the Greeks. It gave to the young men good looks, good health, and good spirits ; it made their limbs nimble, graceful and well-formed ; in their souls it lighted the first sparks of the desire for good name, the love of fame even, and stamped on them the inviolable temper of men who live for their city and their country. Finally, what was most precious, it laid the foundation in their characters of that predilection for male society and friendship which so markedly distinguishes the Greeks. In Greece, woman was not the one prize of life for which the young man fought and strove ; the loveliest Helen could only mould the spirit of one Paris, even though her beauty might be the coveted object of all manly valour. The feminine sex, despite the splendid examples of every virtue that it exhibited in Greece, as elsewhere, remained there only a secondary object of the manly life. The thoughts of aspiring youths reached towards something higher. The bond of friendship which they knitted among themselves or with grown men, compelled them into a school which Aspasia herself could hardly have introduced them to ; so that in many of the states of Greece manly love became surrounded and accompanied by those intelligent and educational influences, that permanence of character and devotion, whose sentiment and meaning we read of in Plato almost as if in a romance from some far planet."

ELISAR von Kupffer, in the introduction to his Anthology, from which I have already quoted a few extracts, speaks at some length on the great ethical and political significance of a loving comradeship. He says :—

"IN open linkage and attachment to each other ought youth to rejoice in youth. In attachment to another, one loses the habit of thinking only of self. In the love and tender care and instruction that the youth receives from his lover he learns from boyhood up to recognise the good of self-sacrifice and devotion ; and in the love which he shows, whether in the smaller or the greater offerings of an intimate friendship, he accustoms himself to self-sacrifice for another. In this way the young man is early nurtured into a member of the Community—to a useful member and not one who has self and only self in mind. And how much closer thus does unit grow to unit, till indeed the whole comes to feel itself a whole! . . .

"The close relationship between two men has this further result—that folk instinctively and not without reason judge of one from the other; so that should the one be worthy and honorable, he naturally will be anxious that the other should not bring a slur upon him. Thus there arises a bond of moral responsibility with regard to character. And what can be of more advantage to the community than that the individual members should feel responsible for each other? Surely it is just that which constitutes national sentiment, and the strength of a people, namely, that it should form a complete whole in itself, where each unit feels locked and linked with the others. Such unions may be of the greatest social value, as in the case of the family. And it is especially in the hour of danger that the effect of this unity of feeling shows itself; for where one man stands or falls with another, where glad self-sacrifice, learnt in boyhood, becomes so to speak, a warm-hearted instinct, there is developed a power of incalculable import, a power that folly alone can hold cheap. Indeed, the unconquerable force of these unions has already been practically shown, as in the Sacred Band of the Thebans who fought to its bitter end the battle of Leuctra; and, psychologically speaking, the explanation is most natural; for where one person feels himself united, body and soul to another, is it not natural that he should put forth all his powers in order to help the other, in order to manifest his love for him in every way ? If any one cannot or will not perceive this we may indeed well doubt either the intelligence of his head or the morality of his heart."

RIEDRICH Rückert (1788-1866), Professor of Oriental Literature in Berlin, wrote verses in memory of his friend Joseph Kopp :—

Friedrich Rückert to his Friend

"HOW shall I know myself without thee,
Who knew myself as part of thee ?
I only know one half is vanished,
And half alone is left, of me.
Never again my proper mind
I'll know ; for thee I'll never find.

Never again, out there in space,
I'll find thee ; but here, deep within.
I see, tho' not in dreams, thy face ;
My waking eyes thy presence win,
And all my thought and poesy
Are but my offering to thee.

. . . . . .

Modern Times

My Jonathan, now hast thou fled,
And I to weep thy loss remain;
If David's harp might grace my hands
O might it help to ease my pain!
My friend, my Joseph, true of faith,
In life so loved—so loved in death."

And the following are by Joseph Kitir, an
Austrian poet:—

"NOT where breathing roses bless
The night, or summer airs caress;
Not in Nature's sacred grove;
No, but at a tap-room table,
Sitting in the window-gable
Did we plight our troth of love.

No fair lime tree's roofing shade
By the spring wind gently swayed
Formed for us a bower of bliss;
No, stormbound, but love-intent,
There against the damp wall bent
We two bartered kiss for kiss.

Therefore shalt thou, Love so rare
(Child of storms and wintry air),
Not like Spring's sweet fragrance fade.
Even in sorrow thou shalt flourish,
Frost shall not make thee afraid,
And in storms thou shalt not perish."

213

O N p. 154, 155 above are given some letters of Richard Wagner relative to Ludwig II.'s deep attachment to him. Below are some of the actual letters of Ludwig to Wagner. (See Prof. C. Beyer's book, *Ludwig II., König von Bayern.*)

Ludwig II. to Richard Wagner "DEAR Friend, O I see clearly that your sufferings are deep-rooted! You tell me, beloved friend, that you have looked deep into the hearts of men, and seen there the villainy and corruption that dwells within. Yes, I believe you, and I can well understand that moments come to you of disgust with the human race; yet always will we remember (will we not, beloved?) that there are yet many noble and good people, for whom it is a real pleasure to live and work. And yet you say you are no use for this world!—I pray you, do not despair, your true friend conjures you; have Courage: 'Love helps us to bear and suffer all things, love brings at last the victor's crown!' Love recognises, even in the most corrupt, the germ of good; she alone overcomes all!—Live on, darling of my soul. I recall your own words to you. To learn to forget is a noble work!—Let us be careful to hide the faults of others ; it was for all men indeed that the Saviour died and suffered. And now, what a pity that 'Tristan' can not be presented to-day ; will it perhaps to-morrow ? Is there any chance ?

Unto death your faithful friend,
15*th May*, 1865. LUDWIG."

"*Purschling*, 4*th Aug*., 1865.

'MY one, my much-loved Friend,—You express to me your sorrow that, as it seems to you, each one of our last meetings has only brought pain and anxiety to me.—Must I then remind my loved one of Brynhilda's words ?— Not only in gladness and enjoyment, but in suffering also Love makes man blest. . . . When does my friend think of coming to the 'Hill-Top,' to the woodland's aromatic breezes ? —Should a stay in that particular spot not altogether suit, why, I beg my dear one to choose any of my other mountain-cabins for his residence. —What is mine is his ! Perhaps we may meet on the way between the Wood and the World, as my friend expressed it ! . . . To thee I am wholly devoted ; for thee, for thee only to live !

Unto death your own, your faithful
LUDWIG."

"*Hohenschwangau, 2nd Nov.,* 1865.

"MY one Friend, my ardently beloved ! This afternoon, at 3.30, I returned from a glorious tour in Switzerland ! How this land delighted me !—There I found your dear letter ; deepest warmest thanks for the same. With new and burning enthusiasm has it filled me ; I see that the beloved marches boldly and confidently forward, towards our great and eternal goal.

"All hindrances I will victoriously like a hero overcome. I am entirely at thy disposal ; let me now dutifully prove it.—Yes, we must meet and speak together. I will banish all evil clouds ; Love has strength for all. You are the star that shines upon my life, and the sight of you ever wonderfully strengthens me.—Ardently I long for you, O my presiding Saint, to whom I pray ! I should be immensely pleased to see my friend here in about a week ; oh, we have plenty to say ! If only I could quite banish from me the curse of which you speak, and send it back to the deeps of night from whence it sprang !—How I love, how I love you, my one, my highest good ! . . .

"My enthusiasm and love for you are boundless. Once more I swear you faith till death !

Ever, ever your devoted
LUDWIG."

Modern Times

BYRON'S "Death of Calmar and Orla: an Imitation of Ossian," is, like his "Nisus and Euryalus" (see above, p. 163), a story of two hero-friends who, refusing to be separated, die together in battle :—

"IN Morven dwelt the chief; a beam of war to *Byron's* Fingal. His steps in the field were marked *Calmar* in blood. Lochlin's sons had fled before his *and Orla* angry spear; but mild was the eye of Calmar; soft was the flow of his yellow locks: they streamed like the meteor of the night. No maid was the sigh of his soul: his thoughts were given to friendship—to dark-haired Orla, destroyer of heroes! Equal were their swords in battle; but fierce was the pride of Orla—gentle alone to Calmar. Together they dwelt in the cave of Oithona." [Orla is sent by the King on a mission of danger amid the hosts of the enemy. Calmar insists on accompanying him, in spite of all entreaties to the contrary. They are discovered. A fight ensues, and they are slain.] "Morn glimmers on the hills: no living foe is seen; but the sleepers are many; grim they lie on Erin. The breeze of ocean lifts their locks;

yet they do not awake. The hawks scream above their prey.

"Whose yellow locks wave o'er the breast of a chief? Bright as the gold of the stranger they mingle with the dark hair of his friend. 'Tis Calmar: he lies on the bosom of Orla. Theirs is one stream of blood. Fierce is the look of gloomy Orla. He breathes not, but his eye is still aflame. It glares in death unclosed. His hand is grasped in Calmar's; but Calmar lives! He lives, though low. 'Rise,' said the King, 'Rise, son of Mora: 'tis mine to heal the wounds of heroes. Calmar may yet bound on the hills of Morven.'

"'Never more shall Calmar chase the deer of Morven with Orla,' said the hero. 'What were the chase to me alone? Who should share the spoils of battle with Calmar? Orla is at rest. Rough was thy soul, Orla! Yet soft to me as the dew of morn. It glared on others in lightning: to me a silver beam of night. Bear my sword to blue-eyed Mora; let it hang in my empty hall. It is not pure from blood: but it could not save Orla. Lay me with my friend. Raise the song when I am dead.'" [So they are laid by the stream of Lubar, and four gray stones mark the dwelling of Orla and Calmar.]

Modern Times

ERNST Hæckel, in his " Visit to Ceylon" describes the devotion entertained for him by his Rodiya serving-boy at Belligam, near Galle. The keeper of the rest-house at Belligam was an old and philosophically-minded man, whom Hæckel, from his likeness to a well known head, could not help calling by the name of Socrates. And he continues :—

"IT really seemed as though I should be pursued by the familiar aspects of classical antiquity from the first moment of my arrival at my idyllic home. For, as Socrates led me up the steps of the open central hall of the rest-house, I saw before me, with uplifted arms in an attitude of prayer, a beautiful naked brown figure, which could be nothing else than the famous statue of the 'Youth adoring.' How surprised I was when the graceful bronze statue suddenly came to life, and dropping his arms fell on his knees, and, after raising his black eyes imploringly to mine, bowed his handsome face so low at my feet that his long black hair fell on the floor ! Socrates informed me that this boy was a Pariah, a member of the lowest caste, the Rodiyas,

Hæckel's Visit to Ceylon

219

who had lost his parents at an early age, so he had taken pity on him. He was told off to my exclusive service, had nothing to do the livelong day but obey my wishes, and was a good boy, sure to do his duty punctually. In answer to the question what I was to call my new body-servant, the old man informed me that his name was Gamameda. Of course I immediately thought of Ganymede, for the favorite of Jove himself could not have been more finely made, or have had limbs more beautifully proportioned and moulded. As Gamameda also displayed a peculiar talent as butler, and never allowed anyone else to open me a cocoa-nut or offer me a glass of palm wine, it was no more than right that I should dub him Ganymede.

His   "Among the many beautiful figures which move
Rodiya in the foreground of my memories of the para-
Boy dise of Ceylon, Ganymede remains one of my dearest favorites.   Not only did he fulfil his duties with the greatest attention and conscientiousness, but he developed a personal attachment and devotion to me which touched me deeply. The poor boy, as a miserable outcast of the Rodiya caste, had been from his birth the object of the deepest contempt of his fellow-men, and

subjected to every sort of brutality and ill-treatment. With the single exception of old Socrates, who was not too gentle with him either, no one perhaps had ever cared for him in any way. He was evidently as much surprised as delighted to find me willing to be kind to him from the first. . .
. . . I owe many beautiful and valuable contributions to my museum to Ganymede's unfailing zeal and dexterity. With the keen eye, the neat hand, and the supple agility of the Cinghalese youth, he could catch a fluttering moth or a gliding fish with equal promptitude ; and his nimbleness was really amazing, when, out hunting, he climbed the tall trees like a cat, or scrambled through the densest jungle to recover the prize I had killed." *My Visit to Ceylon, by Ernst Hæckel*, p. 200. (Kegan Paul, Trench & Co., 1883).

Hæckel stayed some weeks in and around Belligam ; and continues, (p. 272) :—

"ON my return to Belligam I had to face one of the hardest duties of my whole stay in Ceylon : to tear myself away from this lovely spot of earth, where I had spent six of the happiest and most interesting weeks in my life.
. . . But hardest of all was the parting from

my faithful Ganymede ; the poor lad wept bitterly, and implored me to take him with me to Europe. In vain had I assured him that it was impossible, and told him of our chill climate and dull skies. He clung to my knees and declared that he would follow me unhesitatingly wherever I would take him. I was at last almost obliged to use force to free myself from his embrace. I got into the carriage which was waiting, and as I waved a last farewell to my good brown friends, I almost felt as if I had been expelled from Paradise."

EDWARD Fitzgerald, the interpreter and translator of *Omar Khayyam*, was a man of the deepest feeling and sensibility, with a special gift for friendship. Men like Tennyson and Thackeray declared that they loved him best of all their friends. He himself said in one of his letters " My friendships are more like loves." A. C. Benson, his biographer, writes of him :—

"HE was always taking fancies, and once under the spell he could see no faults in his friend. His friendship for Browne arose out of *Edward* one of these romantic impulses. So too his *Fitz-* affection for Posh, the boatman; for Cowell, and *gerald's* for Alfred Smith, the farmer of Farlingay and *friendship* Boulge, who had been his protégé as a boy. He seems to have been one of those whose best friendships are reserved for men; for though he had beloved women friends like Mrs. Cowell and Mrs. Kemble, yet these are the exceptions rather than the rule. The truth is, there was a strong admixture of the feminine in Fitzgerald's character." *Fitzgerald, English Men of Letters Series*, ch. viii.

The friendship with Posh, the fisherman, at Lowestoft and at Woodbridge, lasted over many years. Fitzgerald had a herring-lugger built for him, which he called the *Meum and Tuum*, and in which they had many a sail together. Benson, speaking of their first meeting, says:—

"IN the same year [1864] came another great *Fitz-* friendship. He made the acquaintance of a *gerald* stalwart sailor named Joseph Fletcher, commonly *and Posh* called Posh. It was at Lowestoft that he was found, where Fitzgerald used, as he wrote in

1850, 'to wander about the shore at night longing
for some fellow to accost me who might give
some promise of filling up a very vacant place
in my heart.' Posh had seen the melancholy
figure wandering about, and years after, when
Fitz used to ask him why he had not been
merciful enough to speak to him, Posh would
reply that he had not thought it becoming.
Posh was, in Fitzgerald's own words, 'a man of
the finest Saxon type, with a complexion, *vif*,
mâle et flamboyant, blue eyes, a nose less than
Roman, more than Greek, and strictly auburn
hair that woman might sigh to possess.' He
was too, according to Fitz, 'a man of simplicity
of soul, justice of thought, tenderness of nature,
a gentleman of Nature's grandest type.' Fitz
became deeply devoted to this big-handed, soft-
hearted, grave fellow, then 24 years of age."

Ibid, ch. iii.

Index

INDEX

Index

Index

Index

Index

230

Index

231

Index

Index

233

Index

Index